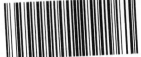

YUBISASHI®

H

この本の使い方

step 1

Point at the word you intend to express.

Just point at the word and show to the other person. Try pronouncing out loud. He/She should show interest.

step 2

You can combine words and create phrases.

For example, you can point to "Where is~?"and then "restaurant". You have just created a question "Where is the restaurant?" The secret is to point slowly.

step 3

Encourage the other party to also point at the words.

私と同じように、言葉を指して答えてくださいね。
(translation : Please point at the word/s and answer me, just like I do.)

Japanese ·Top20 Basic Phrases

Shoping,eating, and more!
These wards are useful & needful !!

20
日本語
超基本フレーズ

Greetings · How to greet others あいさつ・呼びかけの言葉

Hello.
こんにちは
konnichiwa

Excuse me.
すみません
sumimasen

Good morning.
おはようございます
ohayoo gozaimasu

Good evening.
こんばんは
konbanwa

How do you do. Nice to meet you.
はじめまして、お会いできてうれしいです
hajimemashite, oaidekite ureshii desu

Thank you.
ありがとう
arigatoo

You're welcome.
どういたしまして
dooitashimashite

Good bye.
さようなら
sayoonara

(I'm) sorry.
ごめんなさい
gomen nasai

How to ask for favors お願いする言葉

Please see this book.
この本を見てください
kono hon o mite kudasai

Could you take some photos for me?
写真を撮ってください
shashin o totte kudasai

Please write it down.
書いてください
kaite kudasai

Asking for directions 場所・行き方をたずねる言葉

Where is the~?
～はどこですか？
wa doko desu ka

I want to go to ~.
～に行きたい
ni ikitai

convenience store コンビニ kombini	**station** 駅 eki	**bank** 銀行 ginkoo
restroom トイレ toire	**entrance** 入口 iriguchi	**exit** 出口 deguchi

Useful money-related phrases
便利なお金フレーズ

How much is it?
いくらですか？
ikura desu ka

I'll have this.
これをください
kore o kudasai

0 零 rei/zero	1 一 ichi	2 二 ni
3 三 san	4 四 yon/shi	5 五 go
6 六 roku	7 七 nana/shichi	8 八 hachi
9 九 kyuu	10 十 juu	20 二十 nijuu

Any discount?
少し安くなりませんか？
sukoshi yasuku narimasen ka

Is this duty-free?
免税品ですか？
menzee hin desu ka

Can I use?
使えますか？
tsukaemasu ka

Which dollar is this?
どこのドルですか？
dokono doru desuka

credit card
クレジットカード
kurejitto kaado

dollar
ドル
doru

traveler's checks
トラベーラーズ チェック
toraberaazu chekku

Can you exchange?
両替できますか
ryoogae dekimasu ka

rate
レート
reeto

You can just point at the price here
値段は、指さしてもらえば OK !

1 yen 一円
ichi en

5 yen 五円
go en

10 yen 十円
juu en

I often receive as small change. I want to use them so that they won't pile up.
おつりでもらうことが多い。すぐたまるのでこまめに使おう。

50 yen 五十円
gojuu en

Widely used domestic postcard is 50 yen.
日本国内で使える、一般的な郵便はがきが50円。

100 yen 百円
hyaku en

Chewing gum, icecream, rice-balls are about 100 yen.
ガムやアイス、おにぎりなどがだいたい100円。

500 yen 五百円
gohyaku en

Beef on rice, Tako-Yaki, and light snacks are about 500 yen.
牛丼やたこ焼き、軽食などは500円前後で食べられる。

1,000 yen 千円
sen en

Paper money is easier to use, fit for all occasions.
シチュエーション問わず、使い勝手のよい紙幣。

2,000 yen 弐千円
nisen en

Issued to commemorate the 2000 Okinawa G8 Summit.
2000年沖縄サミットを記念して発行。あまり流通していない。

5,000 yen 五千円
gosen en

Widely used for paying meals and for shopping.
夕食や買い物のときなどによく使う紙幣。

10,000 yen 壱万円
ichiman en

Not recommended using in small stores and taxis; they may not have change.
小さな店やタクシーなどで使うと、相手がおつりに困ることも。

CONTENTS

Airport/Hotel

Baggage's lost! What can I say?

I can't find my baggage.
荷物が出てきません
nimotsu ga dete kimasen

Lost checked-in baggage sometimes happens. Don't panic and ask the airline personnel.

機内預けの荷物が出てこないトラブルは今でもときどきあります。そんなときは焦らず職員にたずねてみてください。

It's important to verify the time.

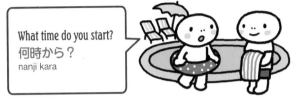

What time do you start?
何時から？
nanji kara

There's a time restraint on meal time and use of the swimming pool. Use this phrase to verify the correct time.

旅館の食事やホテルのプールなどは時間が決められていることも。時間の確認はこのフレーズで。

This doesn't fit.

Do you have a larger size?
もっと大きいものはありますか？
motto ookii mono wa arimasu ka

Hotel Yukata and sandals often come too small. To inquire about how to wear the kimono and how to take the bath, please see Page 15.

宿の浴衣や履き物が小さかったらこのフレーズを。浴衣の着方や風呂の入り方をたずねる言葉は15ページにあります。

Airport 空港

Immigration

purpose of stay
滞在目的
taizai mokuteki

Sightseeing
観光です
kankoo desu

business
仕事
shigoto

studying abroad
留学する
ryuugaku suru

Working holiday
ワーキングホリデー
waakingu horidee

I live in Japan.
日本に住んでいます
nihon ni sunde imasu

return ticket
帰りの航空券
kaeri no kookuu ken

length of stay
滞在期間
taizai kikan

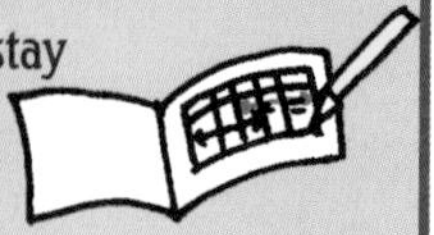

about
だいたい
daitai

1 week
１週間
isshuu kan

2 weeks
２週間
nishuu kan

1 month
１ヵ月
ikka getsu

1 year
１年
ichi nen

Customs

items to declare
申告するもの
shinkoku suru mono

I have some.
あります
arimasu

I don't have any.
ありません
arimasen

Interpreter, please.
通訳を呼んでください
tsuuyaku o yonde kudasai

Please speak slowly.
ゆっくり話してください
yukkuri hanashite kudasai

Where is the ~?
~はどこですか？
wa doko desu ka

Excuse me.
すみません
sumimasen

baggage claim 荷物受取所 nimotsu uketori jo	**cart** カート kaato	**restroom** トイレ toire
information desk 案内所 annai jo	**currency exchange** 両替所 ryoogae jo	**duty free shop** 免税店 menzee ten
transfer 乗り継ぎ nori tsugi	**departure counter** 出発カウンター shuppatsu kauntaa	**boarding gate** 搭乗ゲート toojoo geeto

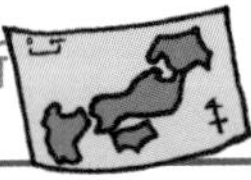

International flights 国際線 kokusai sen	**Domestic flights** 国内線 kokunai sen

When do you start boarding?
搭乗開始時間は何時ですか？
toojoo kaishi jikan wa nanji desu ka

Wi-Fi Wi-Fi waifai	**SIM card** SIMカード shimu kaado

Trouble

I can't find my baggage. 荷物が出てきません nimotsu ga dete kimasen	**My bag is broken.** 荷物が壊れています nimotsu ga kowarete imasu

Stay in a Hotel ホテル滞在

Do you have a reservation?
ご予約されていますか？
goyoyaku sarete imasu ka

I have a reservation under the name ~.
~の名前で予約しています
no namae de yoyaku shite imasu

Do you have any rooms available?
部屋は空いていますか?
heya wa aite imasu ka

I don't have a reservation.
予約していません
yoyaku shite imasen

single room
シングル
shinguru

I made a reservation on the Internet.
ネットで予約しました
netto de yoyaku shimashita

double room
ダブル
daburu

twin room
ツイン
tsuin

I have already paid with my credit card.
カードで支払い済みです
kaado de shiharai zumi desu

stay for~nights
□泊
haku

~person/s
□人
nin

*Numbers →P43

How much is it?
いくらですか？
ikura desu ka

What time do you start?
何時から？
nanji kara

What time do you close?
何時まで？
nanji made

breakfast
朝食
choo shoku

shop
売店
bai ten

restaurant
レストラン
resutoran

room service
ルームサービス
ruumu saabisu

Is there a ~ near here?
この近くに~はありますか？
kono chikaku ni~wa arimasu ka

bank
銀行
ginkoo

convenience store
コンビニ
kombini

Internet cafe
ネットカフェ
netto kafe

station
駅
eki

Can you tell me how to get there?
行き方を教えてください
iki kata o oshiete kudasai

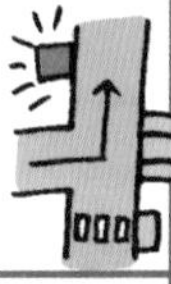

Trouble

It's broken.
壊れています
kowarete imasu

Please write it down.
書いてください
kaite kudasai

air conditioner
エアコン
eakon

TV
テレビ
terebi

refrigerator
冷蔵庫
reezooko

lights
電気
denki

shower
シャワー
shawaa

restroom
トイレ
toire

Could you show me how to use Wi-Fi?
Wi-Fiの使い方を教えてください
waifai no tsukaikata o oshiete kudasai

Call a taxi, please.
タクシーを呼んでください
takushii o yonde kudasai

Could you keep this luggage?
荷物を預かってくれますか？
nimotsu o azukatte kure masuka

Japanese-Style Inn 旅館

Thank you for your help.
お世話になります
osewa ni narimasu

Welcome.
いらっしゃいませ
irasshai mase

Please take off shoes here.
靴はここで脱いでください
kutsu wa koko de nuide kudasai

I will take you to your room.
お部屋に案内します
oheya ni annai shimasu

Where is the ~?
~はどこですか？
wa doko desu ka

This is~.
ここが~です
koko ga~desu

Open-air Spa
露天風呂
roten buro

Reserved Private Spa
貸切風呂
kashikiri buro

dining room
食事処
shokuji dokoro

common bathing area
大浴場
dai yokujoo

men's section
男湯
otoko yu

women's section
女湯
onna yu

What time do you open?
何時から？
nanji kara

What time do you close?
何時まで？
nanji made

breakfast
朝食
chooshoku

dinner
夕食
yuushoku

meal in your room
部屋食
heya shoku

May I help you?
何かお困りですか？
nanika okomari desu ka

Just a moment.
少々お待ちください
shoo shoo omachi kudasai

Teach me how to wear the Yukata.
浴衣の着方を教えてください
yukata no kikata o oshiete kudasai

Is there a larger size?
大きいサイズはありますか？
ookii saizu wa arimasu ka

This is the largest.
これが一番大きいです
kore ga ichiban ookii desu

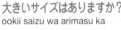

Teach me how to use the bath.
風呂の使い方を教えてください
furo no tsukaikata o oshiete kudasai

Wash your body before you soak in the bathtub.
湯船につかる前に体を洗ってください
yubune ni tsukaru mae ni karada o aratte kudasai

Do not put your towel inside the bathtub.
タオルを湯船に入れないでください
taoru o yubune ni irenai de kudasai

Thank you for your good service.
お世話になりました
osewa ni narimashita

Please come again.
またお越しください
mata okoshi kudasai

Moving

Basic phrase when you want to start a conversation.

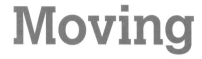

Excuse me.
すみません
sumimasen

Basically shy Japanese will respond positively when you talk with this Show & Talk Book!

恥ずかしがり屋の日本人も、この本を見せながら話しかければ応えやすいはず！

Don't know which ticket to buy.

How can I buy tickets?
きっぷの買い方を教えてください
kippu no kaikata o oshiete kudasai

The railway system in the big city is convenient, but can be very complex. Use this phrase when you want to learn how to buy tickets.

電車は安くて便利な交通機関ですが、大都市では路線も多く複雑です。きっぷの買い方がわからないときはこのフレーズを。

When a Japanese talk to you like this.

I can take you there.
私が案内します
watashi ga annai shimasu

Some Japanese believe that it's easier to just escort you rather than giving you directions. Just accept his/her kindness and follow.

英語で説明するより一緒に行った方が早い、という日本人もいます。そんなときは遠慮せずに案内してもらいましょう。

Walk Around 歩く

I want to go to ~.
～に行きたい
ni ikitai

Where are we?
ここはどこですか？
koko wa doko desu ka

Can you show me on the map?
地図で教えてください
chizu de oshiete kudasai

Please write it down.
書いてください
kaite kudasai

convenience store
コンビニ
kombini

Internet cafe
ネットカフェ
netto kafe

100-yen shop
100円ショップ
hyaku en shoppu

Japanese-style bar
居酒屋
izakaya

bank
銀行
ginkoo

post office
郵便局
yuubinkyoku

restroom
トイレ
toire

station
駅
eki

police station
交番
kooban

This adress
この住所
kono juusho

Where is the closest~?
一番近くの～はどこですか？
ichiban chikaku no~wa doko desu ka

I can take you there.
私が案内します
watashi ga annai shimasu

Let's go together.
一緒に行きましょう！
issho ni iki mashoo

I can teach you the way.
行き方を教えます
iki kata o oshiemasu

Show me your guide book.
ガイドブックを見せて
gaido bukku o misete

straight ahead
まっすぐ
massugu

cross
わたる
wataru

intersection
交差点
koosaten

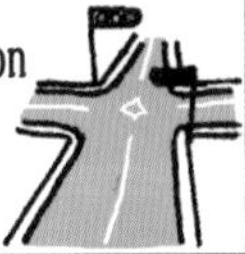

turn right
右折
usetsu

turn left
左折
sasetsu

traffic light
信号
shingoo

first
１つめ
hitotsu me

second
２つめ
futatsu me

third
３つめ
mittsu me

fourth
４つめ
yottsu me

It's about~minutes on foot.
歩いて～分くらいです
aruite~fun kurai desu

1 ichi	3 san	5 go
10 juu	20 nijuu	30 sanjuu

Better take the taxi.
タクシーで行ったほうがいい
takushii de itta hooga ii

Train/Subway 電車・地下鉄

Where is the~?
～はどこですか？
wa doko desu ka

This way,please.
ご案内します
goannai shimasu

ticket office
きっぷ売り場
kippu uriba

ticket gate
改札
kaisatsu

JR Line platform
ＪＲのりば
jeeaaru noriba

subway platform
地下鉄のりば
chika tetsu noriba

Can you tell me how to buy a ticket?
きっぷの買い方を教えてください
kippu no kaikata o oshiete kudasai

How much is it?
いくらですか？
ikura desu ka

to~station
～駅まで
eki made

I bought the wrong ticket.
きっぷを間違えて買ってしまいました
kippu o machigaete katte shimai mashita

change
おつり
otsuri

fare
運賃
unchin

fare adjustment
精算
seesan

Excuse me.
すみません
sumimasen

I want to go to~.
～に行きたい
ni ikitai

Which railway line?
何線ですか？
nanisen desu ka

Which platform?
何番線ですか？
nanbansen desu ka

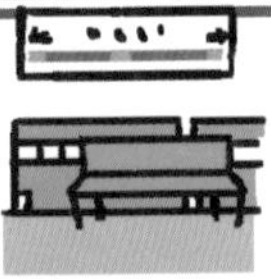

From which track does the train to~departure?
～行きの電車は何番ホームから出ますか？
iki no densha wa nanban hoomu kara demasu ka

What time does the train start?
何時に出発しますか？
nanji ni shuppatsu shimasu ka

What time does it arrive?
何時に着きますか？
nanji ni tsukimasu ka

this train
この電車
kono densha

next train
次の電車
tsugi no densha

the last train
終電
shuuden

Where do you change?
どこで乗り換えですか？
doko de norikae desu ka

Change at~station.
～駅で乗り換え
eki de norikae

Change to the~line.
～線に乗り換え
sen ni norikae

Taxi/Bus タクシー・バス

Taxi

Call a taxi, please.
タクシーを呼んでください
takushii o yonde kudasai

Where's the taxi stand?
タクシー乗り場はどこ？
takushii noriba wa doko

To~ please.
～までお願いします
made onegai shimasu

Go to this address
この住所までお願いします
kono juusho made onegai shimasu

Please tell me when we get to~.
～に着いたら教えてください
ni tsuitara oshiete kudasai

Baggage in the trunk, please.
荷物をトランクに入れてください
nimotsu o toranku ni irete kudasai

Please stop here.
ここで止めてください
kokode tomete kudasai

I'm getting off
降ります
orimasu

How much is it?
いくらですか？
ikura desu ka

Can I pay by credit card?
クレジットカードは使えますか？
kurejitto kaado wa tsukaemasu ka

late night fare
深夜料金
shin ya ryookin

change
おつり
otsuri

receipt
領収書
ryooshuusho

Bus

Where is the~?
～はどこですか？
wa doko desu ka

I want to go to~.
～に行きたい
ni ikitai

bus terminal
バスターミナル
basu taaminaru

bus stop
バス停
basu tee

Going to~
～行きの
iki no

ticket office
チケット売り場
chiketto uriba

pay now
前払い
mae barai

pay later
後払い
ato barai

Does this bus go to~?
このバスは～に行きますか？
kono basu wa~ni ikimasu ka

Which bus should I take?
どのバスに乗ればいいですか？
dono basu ni noreba iidesu ka

What time is the departure?
何時に出発しますか？
nanji ni shuppatsu shimasu ka

What time does it arrive?
何時に着きますか？
nanji ni tsukimasu ka

Is this seat taken?
この席は誰か座っていますか？
kono seki wa dareka suwatte imasu ka

Sightseeing/Culture

To save yourself from the biggest crisis.

Where is the restroom?
トイレはどこですか？
toire wa doko desu ka

Even in resort areas finding restrooms is not that difficult, like in public toilets and inside convenience stores.

公衆トイレやコンビニの店内など、観光地でも街なかでも比較的簡単にトイレは見つかるはず。

Let's make sure to be on the safe side.

Photo taking okay here?
写真を撮ってもいいですか?
shashin o tottemo iidesu ka

Don't snap away in temples and taking photos of Maikos in Kyoto without getting permission first.

お寺の中や京都の舞子さんなどは勝手に写真を撮らず、このフレーズを使って確認しましょう。

You may be able to find hot spots.

Where do you recommend?
どこがおすすめですか?
doko ga osusume desu ka

Ask a local if they know of any hot spots. You may be lucky to be introduced to something not even written in guide books.

地元の人におすすめの観光スポットを聞いてみましょう。ガイドブックには載っていない穴場を紹介してくれるかも。

Sightseeing 観光

I want to go to~.
~に行きたい
ni ikitai

I've been there.
行ったことがあります
itta koto ga arimasu

Tokyo Town Tours
都内観光
tonai kankoo

Yokohama Chinatown
横浜中華街
yokohama chuukagai

Tokyo Disney Resort
東京ディズニーリゾート
tookyoo dizunii rizooto

Universal Studios Japan
ユニバーサル・スタジオ・ジャパン
yuniibaasaru sutajio japan

Mt. Fuji
富士山
fuji san

World Heritage
世界遺産
sekai isan

hot spring
温泉
onsen

Osaka
大阪
oosaka

Kyoto
京都
kyooto

Nara
奈良
nara

Hakata
博多
hakata

Okinawa
沖縄
okinawa

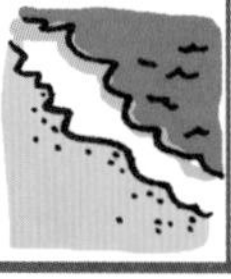

Hokkaido
北海道
hokkaidoo

Where is your favorite place?
あなたのおすすめはどこですか？
anata no osusume wa doko desu ka

Where is the~?
～はどこですか?
wa doko desu ka

ticket office
チケット売り場
chiketto uriba

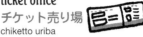

restroom
トイレ
toire

entrance
入口
iriguchi

exit
出口
deguchi

Ticket, please.
チケットをください
chiketto o kudasai

How much is it?
いくらですか?
ikura desu ka

Adult
大人
otona

for children
子供
kodomo

one ticket
1枚
ichi mai

round-trip
往復
oofuku

one-way
片道
katamichi

two tickets
2枚
ni mai

Could you take some photos for me?
写真を撮ってください
shashin o totte kudasai

May I take a photo?
写真をとってもいいですか?
shashin o tottemo iidesu ka

No photos, please!
撮影は禁止です
satsuei wa kinshi desu

No camera flash, please!
フラッシュ禁止です
furasshu kinshi desu

Tourist Attraction in Tokyo 東京の名所

I want to go to~.
～に行きたい
ni ikitai

Where is the~?
～はどこですか？
wa doko desu ka

Tokyo Tower
東京タワー
tookyoo tawaa

TOKYO SKYTREE
東京スカイツリー
tookyoo sukai tsurii

Imperial Palace
皇居
kookyo

Roppongi Hills
六本木ヒルズ
roppongi hiruzu

Sunshine City
サンシャインシティ
sanshain shitii

Tokyo Midtown
東京ミッドタウン
tokyoo middo taun

Kabukicho
歌舞伎町
kabuki choo

Odaiba
お台場
odaiba

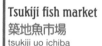

Tsukiji fish market
築地魚市場
tsukiji uo ichiba

The Kabuki Theater
歌舞伎座
kabuki za

Ameyoko Market
アメ横
ameyoko

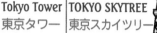

Akihabara Electric Town
秋葉原電気街
akihabara denki gai

Kaminarimon
雷門
kaminari mon

Takeshita Street
竹下通り
takeshita doori

Do you have a tour that goes to~.
～に行くツアーはありますか？
ni iku tsuaa wa arimasu ka

Where should I go?
どこがおすすめですか？
doko ga osusume desu ka

shopping
買い物
kaimono

dining
食事
shokuji

sightseeing
観光
kankoo

Can you teach me?
教えてください
oshiete kudasai

how to get there
行き方
iki kata

regional specialty
名物
meebutsu

tourist attraction
観光名所
kankoo meesho

Where's the nearest station?
最寄り駅はどこですか？
moyori eki wa doko desu ka

What line is it?
何線ですか？
nani sen desu ka

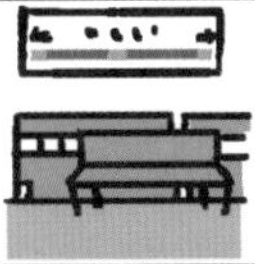

Change at~station.
～駅で乗り換え
eki de norikae

Japanese Culture 日本文化

I want to see~.
～を見たい
o mitai

I want to try~.
～をやってみたい
o yatte mitai

Traditional Culture

Karate
空手
karate

Judo
柔道
juudoo

Kendo
剣道
kendoo

Sumo
相撲
sumoo

Kabuki theater
歌舞伎
kabuki

Noh theater
能
noo

calligraphy
書道
shodoo

Japanese tea ceremony
茶道
sadoo

Shamisen
三味線
shamisen

Zazen
座禅
zazen

Japanese flower arrangement
生け花
ikebana

Kimono wearing lesson
着物の着付け
kimono no kitsuke

cherry blossom viewing
花見
hanami

fireworks shows
花火大会
hanabi taikai

Let's go together!
一緒に行きましょう！
issho ni iki mashoo

I will teach you.
教えてあげます
oshiete agemasu

I want to go to~.
～に行きたい
ni ikitai

Are you interested in~?
～に興味はありますか？
ni kyoomi wa arimasu ka

Pop Culture

Manga Café
マンガ喫茶
manga kissa

Maid Café
メイド喫茶
meedo kissa

Karaoke Bar
カラオケ
karaoke

instant personalized photo stickers
プリクラ
purikura

Game Center
ゲーセン
geesen

Manga
(comic books)
マンガ
manga

anime DVD
アニメDVD
anime diibuidii

figures
フィギュア
figyua

Want the characters of~.
～のキャラクターグッズがほしい
no kyarakutaa guzzu ga hoshii

Akihabara
秋葉原
akihabara

Nakano
中野
nakano

sacred spot
聖地
seechi

~is popular in my country.
私の国では～が人気です
watashi no kuni deha~ga ninki desu

Dining

People would love to hear you say this.

This is good!
おいしい！
oishii

Say something nice in Japanese. No need to speak perfect Japanese.

"味"の感動を日本語で伝えれば、お店の人も喜びます。カタコトでもOKなので言ってみて。

If you know what you want to eat

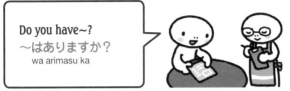

Do you have~?
～はありますか？
wa arimasu ka

Use this phrase when you know what you want. Just add "wa-arimasuka" after the name of the dish.

食べたい料理があるときは、このフレーズで聞いてみましょう。料理名のあとに「～はありますか？」と続けてください。

If you're not sure what to order

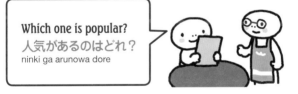

Which one is popular?
人気があるのはどれ？
ninki ga arunowa dore

Popular dishes are featured in the shop's menu. When in doubt ask for the popular item.

人気メニューは、その店の名物料理。注文に迷ったらこのフレーズで人気の一品を聞いてみましょう。

Famous Japanese Food 有名な和食

I'd like to eat~.
～を食べたい
o tabetai

Do you have~?
～はありますか？
wa arimasu ka

Sushi
寿司

vinegared rice with raw or cooked seafood

Tempura
天ぷら

deep-fried seafood and vegetables

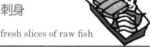

Sashimi
刺身

fresh slices of raw fish

Yakitori
焼き鳥

grilled chicken and vegetables on bamboo sticks

Sukiyaki
すき焼き

beef and vegetables cooked in sweetened soy sauce

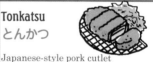

Tonkatsu
とんかつ

Japanese-style pork cutlet

Ramen
ラーメン

Chinese-style noodles in soup

Soba
そば

buckwheat noodles

Udon
うどん
white flour noodles

I've tried before.
食べたことあります
tabeta koto arimasu

I've never tried this.
食べたことがありません
tabeta kotoga arimasen

Let's go eat together!
一緒に食べに行きましょう！
issho ni tabeni iki mashoo

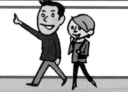

I want to go to~.
～に行きたい
ni ikitai

Which shop do you recommend?
おすすめの店はどこですか？
osusume no mise wa doko desu ka

rotating sushi bar
回転寿司
kaiten zushi

Beef Bowl Shop
牛丼屋
gyuudon ya

family restaurant
ファミレス
famiresu

food stands
屋台
yatai

Japanese-style bar
居酒屋
izakaya

standing pub bar
立ち飲み屋
tachinomi ya

Delicious!
おいしい！
oishii

Not my favorite
苦手
nigate

sweet
甘い
amai

spicy and hot
辛い
karai

salty
しょっぱい
shoppai

sour
すっぱい
suppai

This looks good!
いただきます
itadakimasu

That was good!
ごちそうさま
gochisoosama

Japanese-style bar 居酒屋

~person/s
□人です
nin desu

1	2	3	4	5
ichi	ni	san	yon	go
6	7	8	9	10
roku	nana	hachi	kyuu	juu

Is there a free table?
空いていますか？
aite imasu ka

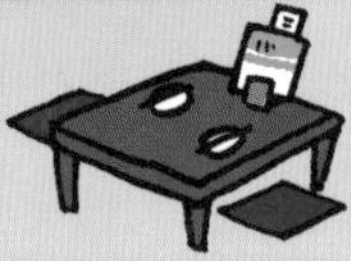

private room
個室
koshitsu

table
テーブル席
teeburu seki

Japanese-style dining section
座敷
zashiki

counter
カウンター
kauntaa

This way, please.
ご案内します
goannai shimasu

Sorry, we're full.
満席です
manseki desu

It's ~minutes wait.
～分待ちになります
fun machi ni nari masu

10	20	30
juu	nijuu	sanjuu
40	50	60
yonjuu	gojuu	rokujuu

May I take your order ?
ご注文はお決まりですか？
gochuumon wa okimari desu ka

I'll have this.
これください
kore kudasai

Which one do you recommend?
おすすめは？
osusume wa

What kind of a dish is this?
これはどんな料理ですか？
kore wa donna ryoori desu ka

Excuse me.
すみません
sumimasen

Can I have~, please.
～ください
kudasai

Where is the restroom?
トイレはどこですか？
toire wa doko desu ka

Your order is not ready yet.
注文した料理がきていません
chuumon shita ryoori ga kite imasen

sake
日本酒
nihonshu

hot sake
熱燗
atsukan

cold sake
冷や
hiya

Shochu (distilled beverage)
焼酎
shoochuu

How do you take your drink?
飲み方はどうしますか？
nomikata wa dooshimasu ka

on the rocks
ロック
rokku

~and water
水割り
mizu wari

shochu with hot water
お湯割り
oyu wari

Check. please.
お会計お願いします
okaikee onegai shimasu

Cheers!
乾杯！
kampai

Please pay at the table.
テーブル会計でお願いします
teeburu kaikee de onegai shimasu

Please pay at the cashier.
レジでお願いします
reji de onegai shimasu

Airport/Hotel
Moving
Sightseeing/Culture
Dining
Shopping
Greetings/Time
Trouble

Light Meal / Drink　軽食・飲み物

Japanese sweets
和菓子
wagashi

Where can I buy it?
どこで買えますか？
doko de kaemasu ka

Taiyaki
たい焼き

bream-shaped pancake with sweet filling

Anmitsu
あんみつ

sweet bean paste parfait

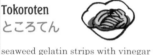

Tokoroten
ところてん

seaweed gelatin strips with vinegar and soy sauce(or black sugar syrup)

Imagawa yaki
今川焼

Japanese pancake with red bean paste

Dorayaki
どら焼き

round sponge cake with sweet bean paste

Yookan
ようかん

sweet bean paste jelly

Monaka
もなか

crisp wafer with red bean paste

shaved ice
かき氷
kakigoori

Senbei
せんべい

Japanese-style rice crackers

Ningyoo yaki
人形焼き

doll-shaped pastry

Which one is popular?
どれが人気ですか？
dore ga ninki desu ka

Have you tried it?
食べたことありますか？
tabeta koto arimasu ka

This shop is famous for this.
この店の名物はこれです
kono mise no meebutsu wa kore desu

drinks
飲み物
nomimono

hot
温かい
atatakai

cold
冷たい
tsumetai

coffee
コーヒー
koohii

Black tea
紅茶
koocha

Japanese tea
日本茶
nihon cha

juice
ジュース
juusu

barley tea
麦茶
mugi cha

Oolong tea
ウーロン茶
uuron cha

carbonated drink
炭酸飲料
tansan inryoo

milk
牛乳
gyuunyuu

soy drink
豆乳
toonyuu

sake
日本酒
nihonshu

draft beer
生ビール
nama biiru

low malt beer
発泡酒
happoo shu

plum wine
梅酒
umeshu

Hoppy
ホッピー
hoppii

Shochu Highball
チューハイ
chuuhai

Tea time!
お茶しましょう！
ocha shimashoo

Let's go for a drink!
飲みに行きましょう！
nomini iki mashoo

Shopping

To ask for the price, this is the phrase.

How much is this?
いくらですか？
ikura desu ka

Be sure to confirm prices. For Check-out expressions go to page 42.

商品の値段がわからなかったら確認しましょう。精算時にレジで使う言葉は42ページにまとめてあります。

Electric Discount Store is where you should go.

Any discount?
少し安くなりませんか？
sukoshi yasuku narimasen ka

You may be able to get a discount on many items. It's always worth a try.

家電量販店では値引きしてくれる商品も多いので、ダメもとで聞いてみましょう。

Smaller shops may not be able to accept this.

Credit cards okay?
クレジットカードは使えますか？
kurejitto kaado wa tsukaemasu ka

Smaller shops and bars may not take credit cards. Be sure to confirm prior to entering the shop.

小さな土産屋や居酒屋ではクレジットカードを使えないこともあるので、入店時に確認しておきましょう。

At Check-out /Number レジにて・数字

I'll take this.
これください
kore kudasai

How much is it?
いくらですか？
ikura desu ka

Can I use?
使えますか？
tsukaemasu ka

credit card
クレジットカード
kurejitto kaado

dollar
ドル
doru

euros
ユーロ
yuuro

Electronic Money(E-Money)
電子マネー
denshi manee

Yen Cash only
日本円の現金しか使えません
nihon en no genkin shika tsukaemasen

Not enough money
お金が足りません
okane ga tarimasen

Different amount
金額が違います
kingaku ga chigai masu

change
おつり
otsuri

Official receipt
領収書
ryooshuusho

receipt
レシート
reshiito

Can you gift wrap?
土産用に包んでください
miyage yoo ni tsutsunde kudasai

Can you wrap separately?
別々に包んでください
betsubetsu ni tsutsunde kudasai

How many?	Please write it down.
いくつ？ ikutsu	書いてください kaite kudasai

Numbers

zero 0 rei	one 1 ichi	two 2 ni	three 3 san	four 4 shi/yon
five 5 go	six 6 roku	seven 7 shichi/nana	eight 8 hachi	nine 9 ku/kyuu
ten 10 juu	eleven 11 juu ichi	twelve 12 juu ni	thirteen 13 juu san	fourteen 14 juu yon
fifteen 15 juu go	twenty 20 nijuu	thirty 30 sanjuu	forty 40 yonjuu	fifty 50 gojuu
sixty 60 rokujuu	seventy 70 nanajuu	eighty 80 hachijuu	ninety 90 kyuujuu	one hunred 100 hyaku

two hundred 200 ni hyaku	five hundred 500 go hyaku	one thousand 1000 sen	ten thousand 10000 ichi man

Clothes & Color 服と色

Do you have~?
～はありますか？
wa arimasu ka

This way,please.
ご案内します
goannai shimasu

shirt 	シャツ	shatsu
blouse 	ブラウス	burausu
sweater	セーター	seetaa
T-shirt 	Tシャツ	tiishatsu
sweatshirt	トレーナー	toreenaa
jacket 	ジャケット	jaketto
suit 	スーツ	suutsu
necktie 	ネクタイ	nekutai
handkerchief	ハンカチ	hankachi
pants	ズボン	zubon
jeans 	ジーンズ	jiinzu
skirt 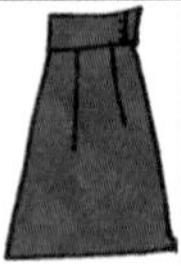	スカート	sukaato
long sleeves	長そで	nagasode
short sleeves	半そで	hansode
sleeveless 	ノースリーブ	noosuriibu
underwear 	下着	shitagi
socks	靴下	kutsu shita
shoes 	靴	kutsu

May I try it on?
試着してもいいですか？
shichaku shitemo iidesu ka

Do you do alterations?
直せますか？
naose masuka

Do you have something more~?
もっと~なものはありますか？
motto~na mono wa arimasu ka

long
長い
nagai

large
大きい
ookii

small
小さい
chiisai

short
短い
mijikai

for men
男性用
dansee yoo

for women
女性用
josee yoo

for children
子供用
kodomo yoo

Colors

white 白 shiro	**black** 黒 kuro	**red** 赤 aka	**blue** 青 ao	**purple** 紫 murasaki
yellow 黄 ki	**green** 緑 midori	**pink** ピンク pinku	**brown** 茶 cha	**beige** ベージュ beeju

I'll take it.
これにします
kore ni shimasu

Where do I pay?
どこで支払えばいいですか？
doko de shiharaeba iidesu ka

Household Electrical Store　家電量販店

Do you have~?
～はありますか？
wa arimasu ka

What floor?
何階ですか？
nan kaki desu ka

This way,please.
ご案内します
goannai shimasu

Sorry, we don't carry.
この店にはありません
kono mise niwa arimasen

personal computer
パソコン
pasokon

computer supplies
パソコン用品
pasokon yoohin

camera
カメラ
kamera

digital camera
デジカメ
dejikame

camcorder
ビデオカメラ
bideo kamera

rice cooker
炊飯器
suihanki

electric shaver
電気かみそり
denki kamisori

wrist watch
腕時計
ude dokee

I want this.
これがほしいです
kore ga hoshii desu

Made where?
どこ製？
doko see

Japan
日本
nihon

South Korea
韓国
kankoku

China
中国
chuugoku

What do you recommend ?
おすすめありますか？
osusume arimasu ka

This is popular.
これが人気です
kore ga ninki desu

This is the latest model.
これが最新モデルです
kore ga saishin moderu desu

Can you use it overseas?
海外で使えますか？
kaigai de tsukaemasu ka

Do you have the instruction book in English?
英語の説明書はありますか？
eego no setsumeesho wa arimasu ka

Is this duty-free?
免税品ですか？
menzeehin desu ka

How do I use it?
どうやって使うんですか？
dooyatte tsukaundesu ka

We will check. Please wait a moment.
調べますので、少々お待ちください
shirabemasunode shooshoo omachi kudasai

Any discount?
少し安くなりませんか？
sukoshi yasuku narimasen ka

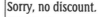

We can give you~yen.
~円までなら安くできます
en made nara yasuku deki masu

Sorry, no discount.
値引きはできません
nebiki wa dekimasen

Japanese Gifts/Comic books 和の小物・マンガ

Do you have~? ～はありますか？ wa arimasu ka	**Where can I buy?** どこで買えますか？ doko de kaemasu ka
This way,please. ご案内します goannai shimasu	**Sorry, we don't carry.** この店にはありません kono mise niwa arimasen

Japanese folding fan 扇子 sensu 	**yukata robe** 浴衣 yukata 	**Japanese character T-shirt** 日本語Tシャツ nihongo tiishatsu
chopsticks はし hashi 	**Japanese wrapping cloth** 風呂敷 furoshiki	**postcard** 絵葉書 ehagaki
chinaware 焼き物 yakimono 	**folk art products** 民芸品 mingeehin 	**Japanese doll** 日本人形 nihon ningyoo
Ukiyoe 浮世絵 ukiyoe	**Ink Painting** 水墨画 suiboku ga	**Food samples** 食品サンプル shokuhin sanpuru 
Japanese umbrella 和傘 wagasa	**sake** 日本酒 nihon shu 	**Japanese tea** 日本茶 nihon cha 

What is this?
これは何ですか？
kore wa nandesu ka

How do I use it?
どうやって使うんですか？
dooyatte tsukaundesu ka

This is most popular in Japan now.
いま日本ではこれが一番人気があります
ima nihon dewa kore ga ichiban ninki ga arimasu

Manga
(Japanese comic book)
マンガ
manga

anime DVD
アニメＤＶＤ
anime diibuidii

figures
フィギュア
figyua

magazines
雑誌
zasshi

anime goods
アニメグッズ
anime guzzu

Cosplay goods
コスプレグッズ
kosupure guzzu

Do you have goods based on~?
～のグッズはありますか？
no guzzu wa arimasu ka

Do you have the English version?
英語版はありますか？
eego ban wa arimasu ka

Sorry, only Japanese.
日本語のみです
nihongo nomi desu

Drugstore/100-yen shop ドラッグストア・100円ショップ

Do you have~? ～はありますか？ wa arimasu ka	**This way, please.** ご案内します goannai shimasu
Just a moment. 少々お待ちください shooshoo omachi kudasai	**Not sold here.** この店にはありません kono mise niwa arimasen

cosmetics 化粧品 keshoohin	**nail polish** マニキュア manikyua	**lipstick** 口紅 kuchibeni
hair products ヘア用品 hea yoohin	**perfume** 香水 koosui	**bath powder** 入浴剤 nyuuyoku zai
shampoo シャンプー shampuu	**conditioner** リンス rinsu	**razor** かみそり kamisori
sanitary napkin 生理用品 seeri yoohin	**diapers** おむつ omutsu	**food supplement** サプリメント sapurimento
cold medicine かぜ薬 keze gusuri	**for men** 男性用 dansee yoo	**for women** 女性用 josee yoo

Is this 100 yen?
これは100円ですか？
korewa hyakuen desu ka

Sorry, this is not 100 yen.
100円ではありません*
hyakuen dewa arimasen

What is this?
これは何ですか？
kore wa nandesu ka

Very popular among tourists.
観光客に人気です
kankookyaku ni ninki desu

fancy stationery
ファンシー文具
fanshii bungu

ballpoint pen
ボールペン
booru pen

mechanical pencil
シャープペン
shaapu pen

Japanese folding fan
扇子
sensu

chopsticks
はし
hashi

Japanese novelties
和小物
wakomono

Japanese Anime goods
アニメグッズ
anime guzzu

CD
CD
shii dii

DVD
DVD
dii bui dii

sweets
お菓子
okashi

calculator
計算機
keesan ki

battery
電池
denchi

sold out
売り切れ
urikire

What's out is our entire stock.
商品は出ているだけです
shoohin wa deteiru dake desu

*Please note. Not all items are priced at 100 yen. 100円ショップといっても、中には100円じゃない商品もあるので要確認!

Greetings/Time

A greeting starts with this word

How do you do?
はじめまして
hajimemashite

Self-introduction phrases are shown on Page 54. Non-English speaking Japanese need not worry with this book.

自己紹介の言葉は54ページにまとめてあります。英語の苦手な日本人でも本を見せれば大丈夫！

Your sincereness speaks more than words.

Thank you.
ありがとう
arigatoo

You can say thank you in Japanese. If the other person thanks you, you can say "Doo itashi mashite".

感謝の気持ちは日本語で伝えましょう。相手に言われたら、「どういたしまして」と返しましょう。

If you want to know how to get in touch with the other person.

Can you tell me?
教えてください
oshiete kudasai

This is how you ask for the email address and postal address. Phrases for asking how to get in touch are outlined on Page 57.

住所やメールアドレスを聞くときはこのフレーズで。連絡先をたずねる言葉は57ページにまとめてあります。

Self Introduction 自己紹介

How do you do?
はじめまして
hajimemashite

Nice meeting you.
お会いできてうれしいです
oai dekite ureshii desu

My name is~.
私の名前は～です
watashi no namae wa~desu

Your name is?
あなたのお名前は？
anata no onamae wa

How old are you?
何歳ですか？
nansai desu ka

I'm~years old.
～歳です
sai desu

Can you speak?
～を話せますか？
o hanase masu ka

Japanese
日本語
nihongo

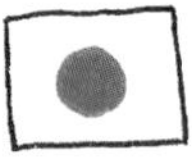

English
英語
eego

Yes, I can speak it.
話せます
hanase masu

No, I cannot speak it.
話せません
hanase masen

Studying now
勉強中
benkyoochuu

I am~. / I work in~.
私は～です
watashi wa~desu

student
学生
gakusee

office worker
サラリーマン
sarariiman

public servant
公務員
koomuin

engineer
エンジニア
enjinia

Where are you from?
出身はどちらですか？
shusshin wa dochira desu ka

I'm from~.
～から来ました
kara kimashita

Why did you come to Japan?
なぜ日本に来たのですか？
naze nihon ni kitano desu ka

sightseeing	studying abroad	business
観光	留学する	仕事
kankoo	ryuugaku suru	shigoto

I will stay in Japan
日本に～います
nihon ni~imasu

~months	~year/years
～ヶ月	～年
kagetsu	nen

First time to Japan.
初めて日本に来ました
hajimete nihon ni kimashita

~time (second time)
～回目です（２回目です）
kaime desu(ni kai me desu)

I came with~.
～と一緒に来ました
to isshoni kimashita

friend
友達
tomodachi

family
家族
kazoku

boyfriend	girlfriend
彼氏	彼女
kareshi	kanojo

Getting acquainted 親しくなる

Tell me about~which you recommend.
あなたのおすすめの～を教えてください
anata no osusume no~o oshiete kudasai

restaurant
レストラン
resutoran

Japanese-style bar
居酒屋
izakaya

Japanese food
和食
washoku

souvenir shop
土産屋
miyageya

tourist attraction
観光名所
kankoomeesho

What kind of person?
どんな人？
donna hito

I/me
私
watashi

you
あなた
anata

cute
かわいい
kawaii

beautiful
きれい
kirei

cool
かっこいい
kakkoii

kind/sweet
やさしい
yasashii

shy
照れ屋
tereya

funny
おもしろい
omoshiroi

talkative
おしゃべり
oshaberi

serious
まじめ
majime

pervert
スケベ
sukebe

Ask for a number to contact

Can you tell me? 教えてください oshiete kudasai	**Please write it down.** 書いてください kaite kudasai

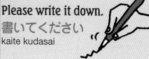

name 名前 namae	**email address** メールアドレス meeru adoresu	**address** 住所 juusho	**phone number** 電話番号 denwa bangoo
Facebook フェイスブック feisu bukku	**Twitter** ツイッター tsuittaa	**letter** 手紙 tegami	**photo** 写真 shashin

I'll send it to you. 送ります okurimasu	**Can you send me?** 送ってください okuttekudasai

This is my address and phone number. 私の連絡先です watashi no renrakusaki desu	**Let's take a picture together.** 一緒に写真を撮りましょう issho ni shashin o tori mashoo
It was nice meeting you. お会いできてよかったです oaidekite yokatta desu	**Hope to see you again.** また会いましょう mata aimashoo

Thank you. ありがとう arigatoo	**You're welcome.** どういたしまして dooitashimashite	**Goodbye!** さようなら sayoonara

Time 時間

What time? 何時ですか？ nanji desu ka	
It's~o'clock. ～時です ji desu	
It's ◯ (o'clock) △ (minutes). ◯時△分です ji fun desu	

10 minutes	20 minutes	30 minutes	40 minutes	50 minutes
10分	20分	30分	40分	50分
juppun	nijuppun	sanjuppun	yonjuppun	gojuppun

about~	~minutes before	~minutes past
～時ごろ	～分前	～分過ぎ
ji goro	fun mae	fun sugi

morning	afternoon	night	midnight
朝	昼	夜	夜中
asa	hiru	yoru	yonaka

morning	afternoon	evening
午前中	午後	夕方
gozenchuu	gogo	yuugata

How long does it take?
どのくらいかかりますか？
donokurai kakari masu ka

~hour
～時間です
jikan desu

It's~minute/s.
～分です
fun desu

Please reserve at~o'clock.
～時に予約を入れてください
ji ni yoyaku o irete kudasai

What time does it leave?
何時に出発しますか？
nanji ni shuppatsu shimasu ka

What time does it arrive?
何時に着きますか？
nanji ni tsuki masu ka

What time does it begin ?
何時に始まりますか？
nanji ni hajimari masu ka

What time does it end ?
何時に終わりますか？
nanji ni owari masu ka

What time should I come?
何時に来ればいいですか？
nanji ni kureba ii desu ka

Please pick me up at~.
～時に迎えに来てください
ji ni mukae ni kite kudasai

Please call a taxi at~.
～時にタクシーを呼んでください
ji ni takushii o yonde kudasai

It's the~o'clock plane.
～時の飛行機です
ji no hikooki desu

Please wake me up at~.
～時に起こしてください
ji ni okoshite kudasai

Month, Day and Year 月日と年月

Weeek

Monday
月曜日
getsuyoo-bi

Tuesday
火曜日
kayoo-bi

Wednesday
水曜日
suiyoo-bi

Thursday
木曜日
mokuyoo-bi

Friday
金曜日
kinyoo-bi

Saturday
土曜日
doyoo-bi

Sunday
日曜日
nichiyoo-bi

When?	○ month △ date
いつ？	○月△日
itsu	gatsu nichi

Months

January
1月
ichi-gatsu

February
2月
ni-gatsu

March
3月
san-gatsu

April
4月
shi-gatsu

May
5月
go-gatsu

June
6月
roku-gatsu

July 7月 shichi-gatsu

August
8月
hachi-gatsu

September
9月
ku-gatsu

October
１０月
juu-gatsu

November
１１月
juu ichi-gatsu

December
１２月
juu ni-gatsu

When did you come to Japan?	When will you return?
いつ日本に来ましたか？ itsu nihon ni kimashita ka	いつ帰りますか？ itsu kaerimasu ka

yesterday	today	tomorrow	~days
昨日 kinoo	今日 kyoo	明日 asu	～日間 nichi kan

last week	this week	next week	~weeks
先週 senshuu	今週 konshuu	来週 raishuu	～週間 shuukan

last month	this month	next month	~months
先月 sengetsu	今月 kongetsu	来月 raigetsu	～ヵ月 kagetsu

last year	this year	next year	~years
去年 kyonen	今年 kotoshi	来年 rainen	～年間 nenkan

Days

1 ichi	2 ni	3 san	4 yon	5 go	6 roku	7 nana	8 hachi
9 kyuu	10 juu	11 juu ichi	12 juu ni	13 juu san	14 juu yon	15 juu go	16 juu roku
17 juu nana	18 juu hachi	19 juu ku	20 nijuu	21 nijuu ichi	22 nijuu ni	23 nijuu san	24 nijuu yon
25 nijuu go	26 nijuu roku	27 nijuu nana	28 nujuu hachi	29 nijuu ku	30 sanjuu	31 sanjuu ichi	

Trouble

Report before you get depressed.

I was robbed!
盗まれた
nusumareta

Japan is a safe country in general, but you never know. When in trouble, report to the police.

日本は治安のよい国ですが油断は禁物。盗難の被害に遭ったら警察に届け出をしましょう。

When you want to give a detailed report.

Interpreter, please.
通訳を呼んでください
tsuuyaku o yonde kudasai

Police or hospital, use this when you need help. Someone who speaks English will come to your aid.

警察や病院で詳しく伝えたいときはこのフレーズを。英語を話せる人が来てくれるはず。

Taking medicine does not improve your condition.

I need a doctor.
医者が必要です
isha ga hitsuyoo desu

When nothing seems to be working, ask the inn keeper to take you to the hospital.

どうにもならないほど体調が悪くなってしまったら、宿の人などに頼んで病院に連れていってもらいましょう。

Robbery/Crime 盗難・犯罪

I was robbed!
盗まれた
nusumareta

I lost it.
なくした
nakushita

Where?
どこで？
doko de

passport
パスポート
pasupooto

cash
お金
okane

wallet/purse
財布
saifu

bag
かばん
kaban

(digital)camera
（デジタル）カメラ
(dejitaru)kamera

airline ticket
航空券
kookuuken

credit card
クレジットカード
kurejitto kaado

traveler's checks
トラベラーズチェック
toraberaazu chekku

I want it reissued.
再発行したい
saihakkoo shitai

I want it canceled.
無効にしたい
mukoo ni shitai

I want a lost report form.
紛失証明書がほしい
funshitsu shoomeesho ga hoshii

Yes, we can.
できる
dekiru

Sorry, we cannot.
できない
dekinai

Interpreter, please.
通訳を呼んでください
tsuuyaku o yonde kudasai

I need a lawyer.
弁護士をつけてください
bengoshi o tsukete kudasai

Help!
助けて！
tasukete

Stop it!
やめて！
yamete

Different types of crime

I was pickpocketed!
スリにあった
suri ni atta

Someone took my bag!
置き引きにあった
okibiki ni atta

I was punched!
殴られた
nagurareta

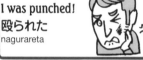

traffic accident
交通事故
kootsuu jiko

Urgent notice

Please contact~.
～に連絡してください
ni renraku shite kudasai

police station
警察
keesatsu

embassy
大使館
taishi kan

ambulance
救急車
kyuukyuu sha

this telephone number
この電話番号
kono denwa bangoo

I have insurance.
保険に入っています
hoken ni haitte imasu

This is my address and phone number.
私の連絡先です
watashi no renraku saki desu

Please don't worry.
安心してください
anshin shite kudasai

Please calm down.
落ち着いてください
ochitsuite kudasai

Drugstores/Clinics 薬局・病院

Is there a drugstore nearby?
薬局は近くにありますか？
yakkyoku wa chikaku ni arimasu ka

Can I have~?
～をください
o kudasai

cold medicine
かぜ薬
kaze gusuri

antidiarrhea medicine
下痢止め
geridome

pain relief
鎮痛剤
chintsuu zai

antacid
胃薬
igusuri

antibiotic
抗生物質
kooseebusshitsu

cough medicine
せき止め
sekidome

Band Aid
ばんそうこう
bansookoo

How should I take this medicine?
この薬はどのように飲みますか？
kono kusuri wa donoyooni nomimasu ka

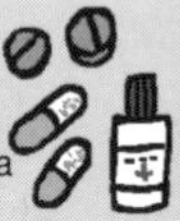

Before meals
食前
shokuzen

~times a day
１日～回
ichi nichi~kai

Take~each time.
１回～錠
ikkai~joo

After meals
食後
shokugo

I'm pregnant.
妊娠しています
ninshin shite imasu

I'm having my period.
生理中です
seerichuu desu

I want to go to the hospital. 病院に行きたいです byooin ni ikitai desu 	**Does he/she speak English?** 英語は通じますか？ eego wa tsuujimasu ka

Examination

body temperature 体温 taion 	**pulse** 脈拍 myaku haku 	**blood pressure** 血圧 ketsu atsu
X-rays レントゲン rentogen 	**injection** 注射 chuusha	**IV** 点滴 tenteki
Past illness 過去の病歴 kako no byooreki	**blood type** 血液型 ketsueki gata	**allergy** アレルギー areruggii

How long will it take to recover?
どのくらいで治りますか？
donokurai de naorimasu ka

Don't worry. 心配いりません shimpai irimasen 	**Rest quietly.** 安静にしてください ansee ni shite kudasai

medical certificate 診断書 shindansho	**prescription** 処方せん shohoosen 	**insurance** 保険 hoken

Explain your symptoms 症状を伝える

Don't feel well 具合が悪い guai ga warui	Want a medicine that works for~. ~に効く薬がほしい ni kiku kusuri ga hoshii

common cold カゼ kaze	have a temperature 熱がある netsu ga aru	feel nauseous 寒気がする samuke ga suru
cough せき seki	stuffy nose 鼻づまり hanazumari	hay fever 花粉症 kafunshoo
headache 頭痛 zutsuu	dizziness めまい memai	anemia 貧血 hinketsu
nausea 吐き気 hakike	heartburn 胸やけ muneyake	no appetite 食欲がない shokuyoku ga nai
diarrhea 下痢 geri	constipation 便秘 bempi	menstrual pain 生理痛 seeri tsuu
feel sluggish だるい darui	sprain ねんざ nenza	burn やけど yakedo

My~hurts. ～が痛い ga itai 		**head** 頭 atama 
eye 目 me 	**ear** 耳 mimi 	**nose** 鼻 hana 
mouth 口 kuchi 	**tooth** 歯 ha 	**throat** のど nodo 
neck 首 kubi 	**shoulder** 肩 kata 	**arm** うで ude 
chest 胸 mune 	**elbow** ひじ hiji 	**back** 背中 senaka 
hand 手 te 	**lower back** 腰 koshi 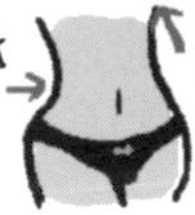	**thigh** もも momo 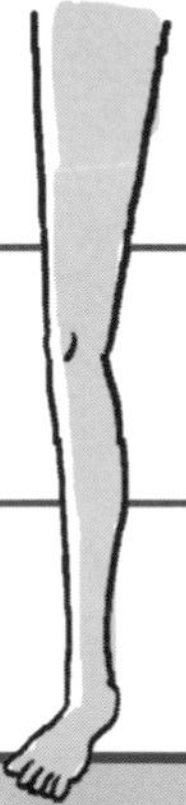
stomach お腹 onaka 	**buttocks** 尻 shiri 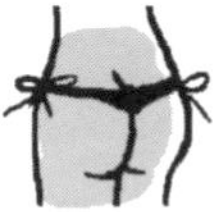	**knee** ひざ hiza
anus 肛門 koomon	**genitals** 性器 seeki	**foot** 足 ashi

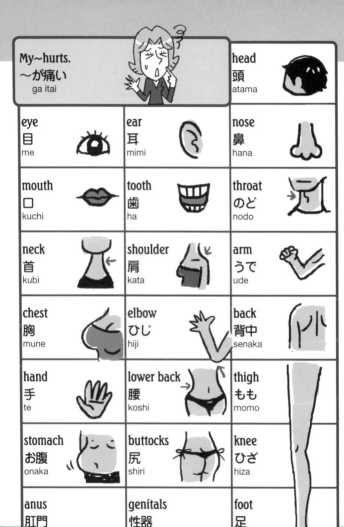

English ››› Japanese

A

a kind/a sort
種類
shurui

a little
すこし
sukoshi

a lot
たくさん
takusan

about
約(およそ)
yaku(oyoso)

above
上
ue

abroad
海外
kaigai

absence
欠席
kesseki

absence
留守
rusu

accept
受け取る
uketoru

accident
事故
jiko

active
活発
kappatsu

actor
俳優
haiyuu

add
加える
kuwaeru

additional prints
焼き増し
yakimashi

address
住所
juusho

admire
感心する
kanshin suru

admission fee
入場料
nyuujoo ryoo

admission ticket
入場券
nyuujoo ken

adult
おとな
otona

adventure
冒険
booken

affection
愛情
aijoo

afternoon
午後
gogo

again
ふたたび
futatabi

age
歳
toshi

agree
賛成
sansee

agriculture
農業
noogyoo

AIDS
エイズ
eizu

air
空気
kuuki

air force
空軍
kuugun

airport
空港
kuukoo

all/everything
すべて
subete

allergy
アレルギー
arerugii

alley/lane
路地
roji

always
いつも
itsumo

ambassador
大使
taishi

This Word Book features 1,500 words most often used by average tourists coming to Japan.

ambulance
救急車
kyuukyuu sha

amusement park
遊園地
yuuenchi

anemia
貧血
hinketsu

animal
動物
doobutsu

ankle
足首
ashikubi

anniversary
記念日
kinenbi

answer
答える
kotaeru

antique
骨董品
kottoo hin

apologize
謝る
ayamaru

appendicitis
盲腸炎
moo choo en

appetite
食欲
shokuyoku

application
申し込み
mooshikomi

application/request
申請
shinsee

April
4月
shi gatsu

architect
建築家
kenchikuka

architecture
建築
kenchiku

arm
腕
ude

army
陸軍
rikugun

arrival time
到着時刻
toochaku jikoku

arrive
到着する
toochaku suru

art
芸術
geejutsu

art craft
民芸品
mingeehin

art museum
美術館
bijutsukan

artist
芸術家
geejutsuka

as usual/as always
相変わらず
aikawarazu

ashtray
灰皿
haizara

aspirin
アスピリン
asupirin

asthma
喘息
zensoku

at a site
現地の
genchi no

at first
最初
saisho

athlete
選手
senshu

atmosphere/feeling
雰囲気
fun iki

attach
貼る
haru

attendance
出席
shusseki

attitude/attractive
魅力的
miryokuteki

August
8月
hachi gatsu

aunt
おば
oba

autumn
秋
aki

B

baby
あかちゃん
akachan

back/spine
背
se

bad
悪い
warui

bag
カバン
kaban

baggage
荷物
nimotsu

bank
銀行
ginkoo

barber shop
理髪店
rihatsuten

baseball
野球
yakyuu

basement
地下
chika

basket
カゴ
kago

bath
風呂
furo

battery
電池
denchi

bay
湾
wan

be born
生まれる
umareru

be broken
こわれる
kowareru

be careful
気をつける
ki o tsukeru

be continued
つづく
tsuzuku

be good at
上手い
umai

be happy
喜ぶ
yorokobu

be late
おくれる
okureru

be on time
まにあう
maniau

bean
豆
mame

beautiful
うつくしい
utsukushii

beauty salon
美容院
biyooin

become dry
乾く
kawaku

become engaged
婚約する
kon yaku suru

bee
蜂
hachi

beef
牛肉
gyuu niku

before
前
mae

begin
はじめる
hajimeru

beginner
初級者
shokyuu sha

behind
後ろ
ushiro

believe
信じる
shinjiru

bet
賭ける
kakeru

Bible
聖書
seesho

bicycle
自転車
jitensha

big
大きい
ookii

bill
紙幣
shihee

bird
鳥
tori

birth control
避妊する
hinin suru

birth control pill
避妊薬
hinin yaku

birthday
誕生日
tanjoobi

bite
噛む
kamu

bitter
にがい
nigai

black
黒い
kuroi

black tea
紅茶
koocha

bladder
膀胱
bookoo

blanket
毛布
moo fu

bleed
出血する
shukketsu suru

blond
金髪
kinpatsu

blood
血
chi

blood pressure
血圧
ketsuatsu

blood test
血液検査
ketsueki kensa

blood type
血液型
ketsuekigata

blossom
咲く
saku

blow
吹く
fuku

blue/green
青い
aoi

boat
船
fune

body
からだ
karada

boil
沸かす
wakasu

boiled
ゆでる
yuderu

book
本
hon

book store
本屋
hon ya

border/edge
国境
kokkyoo

both
両方
ryoohoo

bovine
牛
ushi

box
箱
hako

boxed lunch
べんとう
bentoo

boy
男の子
otoko no ko

brain
脳
noo

break/rest
休憩
kyuukee

breakfast
朝食
choo shoku

breath
息
iki

breathe in
吸う
suu

bride
嫁
yome

bridge
橋
hashi

bright
明るい
akarui

bright (character)
明るい(性格)
akarui(seekaku)

bronchitis
気管支炎
kikanshien

bruise
打撲
daboku

brush (pen)
筆
fude

Buddha statue
仏像
butsuzoo

Buddhism
仏教
bukkyoo

Buddhist
仏教徒
bukkyooto

Buddhist priest/monk
僧侶
sooryo

burglar
強盗
gootoo

burn
燃える
moeru

bus stop
バス停
basutee

busy
いそがしい
isogashii

butterfly
蝶
choo

buy
買う
kau

by the way
ところで
tokorode

C

cafeteria/restaurant
食堂
shokudoo

calculate/figure
計算する
keesan suru

call
呼ぶ
yobu

cancel
とり消す
torikesu

cancer
ガン
gan

candle
ロウソク
roosoku

candy
飴
ame

canned beer
缶ビール
kan biiru

canned food
缶づめ
kanzume

capital city
首都
shuto

car
自動車
jidoosha

cards
トランプ
toranpu

carry
はこぶ
hakobu

cash
現金
genkin

castle
城
shiro

cat
ネコ
neko

catch
つかまえる
tsukamaeru

cause
原因
gen in

cavity
ムシ歯
mushiba

cell phone
携帯電話
keetai denwa

center
中心
chuushin

ceramic
陶器
tooki

certificate of lost item
紛失証明
funshitsu shoomei

chair
いす
isu

change
おつり
otsuri

change
変える
kaeru

change (train/bus/flight)
乗り換える
norikaeru

character/personality
性格
seekaku

charge/fee
手数料
tesuuryoo

cheap/stingy
けち
kechi

check
しらべる
shiraberu

cheek
ほほ
hoho

cherry blossom
サクラ
sakura

chicken
ニワトリ
niwatori

chicken (meat)
トリ肉
tori niku

child
こども
kodomo

childbirth
出産
shussan

childish
こどもっぽい
kodomoppoi

children's clothes
こども服
kodomo fuku

China
中国
chuugoku

Chinese herbal medicine
漢方薬
kanpoo yaku

choose
選ぶ
erabu

chopsticks
箸
hashi

Christian era (A.D.)
西暦
seereki

Christianity
キリスト教
kirisuto kyoo

church
教会
kyookai

cigar
葉巻
hamaki

cigarette
タバコ
tabako

city
市、都市
shi,toshi

city center
都心
toshin

city office
市役所
shiyakusho

civil servant
公務員
koomuin

classy
上品
joohin

clean
そうじ
sooji

clear
澄んだ
sunda

climate
気候
kikoo

climb
登る
noboru

clock/watch
時計
tokee

close
閉める
shimeru

close/shut
閉じる
tojiru

clothing
服
fuku

cloud
雲
kumo

cloudy
曇り
kumori

coffee shop
喫茶店
kissaten

coin
硬貨
kooka

cold
さむい
samui

cold medicine
かぜ薬
kazegusuri

collapse/fall
たおれる
taoreru

collar
エリ(襟)
eri

colleagues
同僚
dooryoo

collect
集める
atsumeru

collide
ぶつかる
butsukaru

color
色
iro

come
来る
kuru

comic
マンガ
manga

commemoration
記念
kinen

company
会社
kaisha

company employee
会社員
kaishain

company president
社長
shachoo

compare
比べる
kuraberu

congratulations
おめでとう
omedetoo

constipation
便秘
benpi

contact lenses
コンタクトレンズ
kontakuto renzu

continue
つづける
tsuzukeru

contract
契約書
keeyakusho

conversation
会話
kaiwa

cook
料理する
ryoori suru

cool
カッコイイ
kakkoii

coral
サンゴ
sango

coral reef
サンゴ礁
sangoshoo

corn
トウモロコシ
toomorokoshi

corner
角
kado

correct
ただしい
tadashii

cosmetics
化粧品
keshoohin

cotton
綿
men

cough
咳
seki

count
数える
kazoeru

country
国
kuni

countryside
いなか
inaka

county
郡
gun

couple
夫婦
fuufu

cow
牛
ushi

crab
カニ
kani

credit card
クレジットカード
kurejitto kaado

crime
犯罪
hanzai

crisis
危機
kiki

cry
泣く
naku

culture
文化
bunka

custom duties
関税
kanzee

cut
切る
kiru

cute
かわいい
kawaii

D

daily goods
日用品
nichiyoohin

dance
踊る
odoru

danger/risk
危険
kiken

dangerous
あぶない
abunai

dark
暗い
kurai

date
日付
hizuke

date of birth
生年月日
seenengappi

daughter
娘
musume

December
12月
juuni gatsu

decide
決める
kimeru

decrease
減る
heru

deep
深い
fukai

definitely
絶対に
zettaini

dehydration
脱水症
dassuishoo

delay/traffic jam
渋滞
juutai

delicious
おいしい
oishii

deliver
配達する
haitatsu suru

demand/request
請求する
seekyuu suru

dentist
歯医者
haisha

depart
発車する
hassha suru

departure time
発車時刻
hassha jikoku

dermatologist
皮膚科
hifuka

desert
砂漠
sabaku

design
模様
moyoo

desire
望み
nozomi

desk
机
tsukue

developing
現像
genzoo

devoted
愛妻家
aisaika

devoted
敬虔な
keiken na

diabetes
糖尿病
toonyoo byoo

diagnosis
診断
shindan

dialect
方言
hoogen

diaper
オムツ
omutsu

diarrhea medicine
下痢どめ
geridome

diary
日記
nikki

dictionary
辞書
jisho

diet
ダイエット
daietto

different
ちがう
chigau

difficult
むずかしい
muzukashii

dig
掘る
horu

diligent
勤勉な
kinben na

dinner
夕食
yuushoku

direction
方向
hookoo

dirty
きたない
kitanai

discount
割引き
waribiki

dish/plate
皿
sara

dislike
きらい
kirai

distance
距離
kyori

dive
潜る
moguru

divide
わける
wakeru

divide
割る
waru

do something
おこなう
okonau

doctor
医者
isha

documents
書類
shorui

dog
犬
inu

doll
人形
ningyoo

domestic line
国内線
kokunaisen

dream
夢
yume

drink
飲む
nomu

drinker
酒飲み
sake nomi

drinking water
飲料水
inryoo sui

drive
運転する
unten suru

driver
運転手
untenshu

driving license
運転免許証
unten menkyoshoo

drop
落とす
otosu

drop of water
水玉
mizutama

dropped item
落とし物
otoshimono

drug store
薬局
yakkyoku

dry cleaning
ドライクリーニング
dorai kuriiningu

dry off
干す
hosu

duck
鴨
kamo

duplicate/spare
合鍵
aikagi

dust
ホコリ
hokori

dusty
ホコリっぽい
hokorippoi

E

ear
耳
mimi

early
早い
hayai

east
東
higashi

easy
簡単
kantan

easy/kind
やさしい
yasashii

education
教育
kyooiku

EENT
耳鼻咽喉科
jibi inkoo ka

effective
有効な
yuukoo na

egg
タマゴ
tamago

elbow
ひじ
hiji

elderly person
老人
roojin

election
選挙
senkyo

electric plug
コンセント
konsento

electricity
電気
denki

elephant
ゾウ
zoo

embarrassed
はずかしい
hazukashii

embassy
大使館
taishikan

embroidery
刺しゅう
shishuu

emergency
緊急
kinkyuu

emergency exit
非常口
hijooguchi

end
終わり
owari

English
英語
eego

enter
入場する
nyuujoo suru

entertainment district
繁華街
hankagai

entrance
入り口
iri guchi

envelope
封筒
fuutoo

equal
等しい
hitoshii

equator
赤道
sekidoo

eraser
消しゴム
keshigomu

errand/business
用事
yooji

escape
にげる
nigeru

ethics
道徳
dootoku

ethnic dance
民族舞踊
minzoku buyoo

ethnic music
民族音楽
minzoku ongaku

ethnic tribe
民族
minzoku

evening
夕方
yuugata

everyone
全員
zen in

everyone
皆(みな)
mina

exact/accurate
正確
seekaku

exactly
ちょうど
choo do

exaggerate
おおげさ
oogesa

example
例
ree

except for ~
~以外
~igai

exception
例外
reegai

exchange
交換する
kookan suru

exchange office
両替所
ryoogaejo

exercise
運動する
undoo suru

exit
出口
deguchi

expect
期待する
kitai suru

expensive
高価
kooka

expensive
高い(値段)
takai (nedan)

experience
経験
keeken

explain
説明する
setsumee suru

express way
高速道路
koosokudooro

extension
内線
naisen

extra incentive
得する
toku suru

eye
目
me

eye drops
目薬
megusuri

F

face
顔
kao

fall
落ちる
ochiru

fall down
ころぶ
korobu

falling star
流れ星
nagare boshi

family
家族
kazoku

family
家庭
katee

famous
有名な
yuumeena

famous spots
名所
meesho

far
遠い
tooi

fashionable
オシャレ
oshare

fast
速い
hayai

father (my)
父
chichi

father/priest
神父
shinpu

feather
毛
ke

February
2月
ni gatsu

fee
費用
hiyoo

feel chilly
寒気
samuke

feel nauseous
吐き気
hakike

feel numb
しびれる
shibireru

feeling
気持ち
kimochi

festival
祭り
matsuri

fever lowering medicine
解熱剤
genetsuzai

fiancé/fiancée
婚約者
kon yaku sha

field
畑
hatake

fight
ケンカする
kenka suru

figure/form
姿
sugatga

filming allowed
撮影可
satsuee ka

filming not allowed
撮影禁止
satsuee kinshi

find
みつける
mitsukeru

finger
指
yubi

finish
終わる
owaru

fire
火
hi

fire extinguisher
消火器
shookaki

first
いちばん
ichi ban

first floor
１階
ikkai

first time
はじめて
hajimete

fish
魚
sakana

fishing
釣り
tsuri

fit
合う
au

flag
旗
hata

flashlight
懐中電灯
kaichuu dentoo

flashy
ハデな
hade na

flat tire
パンク
panku

flood
洪水
koozui

floor
床
yuka

~ floor
~階
~kai

flow
浮く
uku

flower
花
hana

flower vase
花瓶
kabin

flute/whistle
笛
fue

fly
飛ぶ
tobu

fog
霧
kiri

fold
折る
oru

food
食べ物
tabemono

food poisoning
食あたり
shokuatari

foot
足
ashi

for example
たとえば
tatoeba

foreign country
外国
gaikoku

foreign exchange student
留学生
ryuugakusee

forest
森
mori

forever
永久
eekyuu

forget
忘れる
wasureru

fountain pen
万年筆
mannenhitsu

four seasons
四季
shiki

free
無料
muryoo

free time
ひま
hima

free time
余暇
yoka

freeze
こおる
kooru

fresh/new
新鮮
shinsen

Friday
金曜日
kin yoo bi

friend
ともだち
tomodachi

friendship
友情
yuujoo

front
表
omote

fruit
くだもの
kudamono

fry
炒める
itameru

fuel
燃料
nenryoo

full (of people)
満員
man in

fur
毛皮
kegawa

furniture
家具
kagu

future
将来
shoorai

future
未来
mirai

G

gain
得る
eru

garbage
ゴミ
gomi

garbage can
ゴミ箱
gomi bako

garden
庭
niwa

garlic
ニンニク
ninniku

gate
門
mon

get
取る
toru

get angry
怒る
okoru

get drunk
酔う
yo u

get in
入る
hairu

get lost
迷う
mayou

get married
結婚する
kekkon suru

get off
降りる
oriru

get on (a vehicle)
乗る
noru

get together
集まる
atsumaru

get up
起きる
okiru

get well
回復する
kaifuku suru

ghost
オバケ
obake

girl
女の子
onna no ko

give
あげる(人に)
ageru (hito ni)

give birth
産む
umu

glasses
メガネ
megane

globe/earth
地球
chikyuu

go
行く
iku

go out
でかける
dekakeru

go up
上がる
agaru

God
神
kami

gold
金
kin

good
良い
yoi

good at (something)
上手
joozu

good friend
親友
shin yuu

gossip/rumor
うわさ
uwasa

government
政府
seefu

graduate
卒業する
sotsugyoo suru

grandchild
孫
mago

grandfather
祖父
sofu

grandmother
祖母
sobo

grapes
ブドウ
budoo

gray
灰色
haiiro

greed
欲
yoku

green
緑色
midori iro

green grocer
八百屋
yaoya

greeting
あいさつ
aisatsu

ground
地面
jimen

groups
団体
dantai

grow
成長する
seechoo suru

guarantor
保証人
hoshoo nin

guess/imagine
想像する
soozoo suru

guide
案内する
annai suru

gymnastics
体操
taisoo

H

hair
髪
kami

haircut
散髪
sanpatsu

hairdresser
美容師
biyooshi

hand
手
te

hand luggage
手荷物
tenimotsu

hand over
わたす
watasu

handkerchief
ハンカチ
hankachi

happy
うれしい
ureshii

harbor
港
minato

hard
つらい
tsurai

hat
帽子
booshi

have a fever
熱が出る
netsu ga deru

have/hold
持つ
motsu

head
頭
atama

headache
頭痛
zutsuu

health
健康
kenkoo

healthy
元気
genki

heart
心
kokoro

heart
心臓
shinzoo

heat
暖房
danboo

heavy
重い
omoi

height
身長
shinchoo

help
たすける
tasukeru

help
てつだう
tetsudau

hem
スソ(服)
suso(fuku)

hepatitis
肝炎
kan en

her/girlfriend
彼女
kanojo

here
ここ
koko

hero
英雄
eiyuu

hide
かくす、かくれる
kakusu,kakureru

high blood pressure
高血圧
kooketsuatsu

high school
高校
kookoo

hiking
ハイキング
haikingu

hill
丘
oka

him/boyfriend
彼
kare

history
歴史
rekishi

hit (a ball)
打つ
utsu

hobby/interest
趣味
shumi

hold
抱く
daku

hold back
遠慮する
enryo suru

hold in
抱える
kakaeru

hole
穴
ana

holiday
祭日
saijitsu

holiday (day off)
休日
kyuujitsu

hometown
故郷
kokyoo

honesty
正直
shoojiki

honeymoon
新婚旅行
shinkon ryokoo

hope/desire
望む
nozomu

horror story
怪談
kaidan

horse
馬
uma

hospital
病院
byooin

hot
暑い
atsui

hot pepper
トウガラシ
toogarashi

hot springs
温泉
onsen

house
家
ie

housewife
主婦
shufu

housework
家事
kaji

how many
いくつ
ikutsu

how much
いくら
ikura

human
人間
ningen

humidity
湿度
shitsudo

hurry
いそぐ
isogu

husband
夫
otto

I

ice
氷
koori

ID Card
身分証明書
mibun shoomee sho

illness
病気
byooki

imitation
ニセモノ
nisemono

immigration
入管
nyuukan

impossible
不可能
fukanoo

impression
印象
inshoo

independent
独立
dokuritsu

inexpensive
安い
yasui

infant
幼児
yooji

infection
炎症
enshoo

inflation
インフレ
infure

inform
知らせる
shiraseru

information
情報
joohoo

information booth
案内所
annaijo

injection
注射
chuusha

injury
ケガ
kega

insect
ムシ
mushi

insurance
保険
hoken

insurance agency
保険会社
hoken gaisha

intelligent
頭がいい
atama ga ii

interesting
おもしろい
omoshiroi

internal medicine
内科
naika

international line
国際線
kokusai sen

international telephone
国際電話
kokusai denwa

intersection
交差点
koosaten

intestine
腸
choo

introduce
紹介する
shookai suru

invalid
無効
mukoo

invitation card
招待状
shootaijoo

invite
招待する
shootai suru

iron
鉄
tetsu

irony
皮肉
hiniku

Islam
イスラム教
isuramu kyoo

Islamic (person)
イスラム教徒
isuramu kyooto

island
島
shima

issue/publish
発行する
hakkoo suru

it's open
空いている
aite iru

itchy
かゆい
kayui

J

jacket
上着
uwagi

Japan
日本
nihon

Japanese food
日本食
nihonshoku

Japanese language
日本語
nihongo

Japanese sake
日本酒
nihonshu

Japanese yen
日本円
nihon en

July
7月
shichi gatsu

June
6月
roku gatsu

junior high school
中学校
chuugakkoo

K

karate
空手
karate

key
カギ
kagi

kick
ける
keru

kidney
腎臓
jinzoo

kind
親切
shinsetsu

kitchen
台所
daidokoro

kite
凧
tako

knee
ひざ
hiza

knock
ノックする
nokku suru

know
知る
shiru

knowledge
知識
chishiki

Korea
韓国
kankoku

L

laid back
のんき
nonki

lake
湖
mizuumi

land
土地
tochi

landmark
目印
mejirushi

language
言語
gengo

last
最後
saigo

last month
先月
sengetsu

last night
昨晩
sakuban

last week
先週
senshuu

last year
去年
kyonen

late/slow
おそい
osoi

later
あとで
ato de

laugh
わらう
warau

law
法律
hooritsu

lawyer
弁護士
bengoshi

leak
漏れる
moreru

learn
学ぶ
manabu

leave the country
出国
shukkoku

left
左
hidari

letter
手紙
tegami

letter
文字
moji

lie
うそ
uso

light
光
hikari

light (weight)
軽い
karui

light blue
水色
mizuiro

like
好き
suki

like something
気に入る
ki ni iru

like this
このように
kono yoo ni

line
線
sen

lip stick
口紅
kuchibeni

lips
くちびる
kuchibiru

listen
聞く
kiku

lively
にぎやかな
nigiyakana

liver
肝臓
kanzoo

living room
居間
ima

loan
貸す
kasu

local food
郷土料理
kyoodo ryoori

local region
地方
chihoo

long
長い
nagai

long term
長期
choo ki

long time
長い間
nagai aida

look for
探す
sagasu

look good
似合う
niau

look like
似ている
niteiru

lose
なくす
nakusu

lottery
宝くじ
takara kuji

love
愛
ai

luck
運
un

lucky
幸運
kooun

lunch
昼食
chuushoku

lunch time
昼休み
hiru yasumi

lung
肺
hai

M

machine
機械
kikai

made abroad
外国製
gaikokusee

magazine
雑誌
zasshi

mail
郵便
yuubin

make a copy
コピーする
kopii suru

make/give change
両替する
ryoogae suru

male
男性
dansee

man
男
otoko

many
多い
ooi

map
地図
chizu

March
３月
san gatsu

married
既婚
kikon

May
5月
go gatsu

maybe
たぶん
tabun

meal
食事
shokuji

meaning
意味
imi

medical examination
診察
shinsatsu

medical treatment
治療する
chiryoo suru

medicine
薬
kusuri

meet by appointment
待ち合わせ
machiawase

meet with
会う
au

meet/pick up
むかえる
mukaeru

meeting room
待合室
machiai shitsu

member
会員
kaiin

membership card
会員証
kaiinshoo

memorize
考える
kangaeru

memory
思い出
omoide

method
方法
hoohoo

military base/base
基地
kichi

milk
牛乳
gyuu nyuu

mine
私の〜
watashi no

minister
大臣
daijin

minute
分
fun/pun

mirror
鏡
kagami

mistake
まちがい
machigai

molar
奥歯
okuba

Monday
月曜日
getsuyoobi

money
おカネ
okane

monkey
サル
saru

monument
記念碑
kinenhi

moon
月
tsuki

morning
朝
asa

mosquito
蚊
ka

moth
蛾
ga

mountain
山
yama

mouth
口
kuchi

move things
移す
utsusu

move/transfer
移動する
idoo suru

movie
映画
eega

movie theater
映画館
eegakan

muscle
筋肉
kinniku

museum
博物館
hakubutsukan

music
音楽
ongaku

musician
音楽家
ongakuka

mustache/beard
ヒゲ
hige

N

nail
爪
tsume

nail clipper
つめ切り
tsumekiri

naked
はだか
hadaka

name
名前
namae

narrow
せまい
semai

national anthem
国歌
kokka

national flag
国旗
kokki

national park
国立公園
kokuritsu kooen

nationality
国籍
kokuseki

nature
自然
shizen

navy
海軍
kaigun

near
近い
chikai

necessary documents
必要書類
hitsuyoo shorui

neck tie
ネクタイ
nekutai

neighbor
となり
tonari

nephew
おい(甥)
oi

new
新しい
atarashii

New Years
正月
shoogatsu

newlyweds
新婚さん
shinkon san

newspaper
新聞
shinbun

next
次
tsugi

next month
来月
raigetsu

next year
来年
rainen

nice personality
温和な(人柄)
onwa na (hito gara)

nickname
愛称
aishoo

niece
めい(姪)
mei

night
晩
ban

night
夜
yoru

nimble/quick
素早い
subayai

no entry
立入禁止
tachiiri kinshi

no parking
駐車禁止
chuusha kinshi

noisy
うるさい
urusai

non-reserved seat
自由席
jiyuu seki

noodle
麺
men

noon
昼
hiru

normality
正常
seejoo

north
北
kita

nose
鼻
hana

November
11月
juuichi gatsu

now
今
ima

number
数字
suuji

number of people
人数
ninzuu

nurse
看護師
kangoshi

O

obedient/docile
素直
sunao

OBGYN
産婦人科
sanfujinka

observe
見学する
kengaku suru

October
10月
juu gatsu

octopus
タコ
tako

of course
もちろん
mochiron

office
事務所
jimusho

office work
事務職
jimu shoku

oil
油
abura

OK
だいじょうぶ
daijoobu

old
古い
furui

older brother
兄
ani

older sister
姉
ane

oldest daughter
長女
choojo

oldest son
長男
choo nan

on sale
安売り
yasuuri

one day
1日
ichi nichi

one month
1ヵ月
ikka getsu

one time
1回
ikkai

one way
片道
katamichi

one-way street
一方通行
ippoo tsuukoo

one week
1週間
isshuu kan

one's back
腰
koshi

oneself
自分
jibun

onion
タマネギ
tamanegi

only child
ひとりっ子
hitorikko

open sea
沖
oki

operation
手術
shujutsu

ophthalmologist
眼科
ganka

order (restaurant)
注文する
chuumon suru

ordinary
普通
futsuu

Orient/ the East
東洋
tooyoo

origin
原産地
gensanchi

other/back side
裏
ura

out of date
時代遅れ
jidai okure

outside
外
soto

own
所有する
shoyuu suru

owner
持ち主
mochinushi

oyster
かき
kaki

P

package
小包み
kozutsumi

pain
痛い
itai

paint
ペンキ
penki

paint/cover
塗る
nuru

painting
絵画
kaiga

palm
手のひら
tenohira

pan
ナベ
nabe

panties
パンティー
pantii

pants
パンツ
pantsu

paper
紙
kami

parasite/worm
寄生虫
kiseechuu

parents
親
oya

park
公園
kooen

park
駐車する
chuusha suru

parking lot
駐車場
chuushajoo

part
部分
bubun

part time job for students
アルバイト
arubaito

partner
相手
aite

party
宴会
enkai

party
党
too

pass around
回す
mawasu

passenger
乗客
jookyaku

passport number
旅券番号
ryokenbangoo

past
過去
kako

patient
患者
kanja

pay
払う
harau

payment in advance
前払い
maebarai

peace
平和
heewa

pearl
真珠
shinju

peek
のぞく
nozoku

pencil
エンピツ
enpitsu

pension
年金
nenkin

pepper
コショウ
koshoo

perfume
香水
koosui

period
月経
gekkee

permission
許可
kyoka

perspiration
汗
ase

pervert
スケベ
sukebe

pervert
変態
hentai

philosophy
心理学
shinrigaku

photograph
写真
shashin

photography studio
写真屋
shashin ya

pick-pocket
スリ
suri

picnic
ピクニック
pikunikku

picture
絵
e

picture book
絵本
ehon

picture postcard
絵はがき
ehagaki

pillow
まくら
makura

pin number
暗証番号
anshoo bangoo

pizza
ピザ
piza

plan
計画
keekaku

plan
予定
yotee

plant/grass
草
kusa

plants
植物
shokubutsu

plastic/vinyl
ビニール
biniiru

plateau
高原
koogen

play
遊ぶ
asobu

play/theatrical
劇
geki

pleasant
たのしい
tanoshii

pneumonia
肺炎
haien

poem
詩
shi

point
指す
sasu

poison
毒
doku

police
警察
keesatsu

police officer
警察官
keesatsukan

police station
警察署
keesatsusho

polite
ていねい
teenee

politician
政治家
seejika

politics
政治
seeji

pond
池
ike

poor
まずしい
mazushii

poor/no money
貧乏
binboo

popular
流行
ryuukoo

population
人口
jinkoo

pork
ブタ肉
butaniku

positive/active
積極的
sekkyokuteki

possibility
可能性
kanoosee

post office
郵便局
yuubin kyoku

postage
送料
sooryoo

postal code
郵便番号
yuubin bangoo

postcard
はがき
hagaki

poster
はり紙
harigami

postpone
延期する
enki suru

potato
イモ
imo

potato
ジャガイモ
jagaimo

poultice
湿布
shippu

pour into
そそぐ
sosogu

powder
粉
kona

practice
練習する
renshuu suru

praise
ほめる
homeru

pray
いのる
inoru

prediction
予想
yosoo

prefecture
県
ken

pregnancy
妊娠
ninshin

pregnant woman
妊婦
ninpu

prepare
準備する
junbi suru

prepare
用意する
yooi suru

prescription
処方箋
shohoo sen

present
現在
genzai

president
大統領
daitooryoo

press charges
訴える
uttaeru

pretend innocence
とぼける
tobokeru

pretty
きれいな
kirei na

prevent
予防する
yoboo suru

prevent/protect
ふせぐ
fusegu

prevention
防止
booshi

previously/before
すでに
sudeni

price
値段
nedan

price of transportation
運賃
unchin

priest
牧師
bokushi

prime minister
首相
shushoo

print
印刷する
insatsu suru

prison
刑務所
keemusho

private
個人
kojin

private
私立
shiritsu

prize
賞
shoo

procedure
手続き
tetsuzuki

produce
生産する
seesan suru

production
創作
soosaku

professor
教授
kyooju

prohibited
禁止
kinshi

promise
約束
yakusoku

protect/obey
守る
mamoru

protection
保護
hogo

protective charm
お守り
omamori

protest
抗議する
koogi suru

protest
反対する
hantai suru

proverb
ことわざ
kotowaza

proxy
代理人
dairinin

psychiatry ward
精神科
seeshinka

public toilet
公衆トイレ
kooshuu toire

public
公共
kokyoo

public office
役所
yakusho

public phone
公衆電話
kooshuu denwa

public welfare
社会福祉
shakai fukushi

pull
引く
hiku

pull out
抜く
nuku

pulse
脈拍
myakuhaku

pumpkin
カボチャ
kabocha

punch
なぐる
naguru

pure/genuine
純粋
junsui

purple
紫
murasaki

purpose
目的
mokuteki

push
押す
osu

puss/discharge
膿
umi

put away
しまう
shimau

put into
入れる
ireru

put on makeup
化粧する
keshoo suru

Q

qualification
資格
shikaku

quality
品質
hinshitsu

quarantine
検疫
ken eki

question
質問
shitsumon

quiet
おとなしい
otonashii

quit smoking
禁煙する
kin en suru

quotation
見積もり
mitsumori

R

rabbit
ウサギ
usagi

rabies
狂犬病
kyookenbyoo

race/ethnic group
人種
jinshu

railroad
鉄道
tetsudoo

railway track
線路
senro

rain
雨
ame

raise (a child)
そだてる
sodateru

raise/lift (above)
上げる(上に)
ageru (ue ni)

rash/hives
じんましん
jinmashin

rate of exchange
為替レート
kawase reeto

raw
生(なま)
nama

razor blade
カミソリ
kamisori

read
読む
yomu

read books
読書
dokusho

receipt
請求書
seekyuusho

receipt
領収書
ryooshuusho

receive
もらう
morau

recently
最近
saikin

reception
受付
uketsuke

recklessness
無謀
muboo

recognize/approve
みとめる
mitomeru

record/transcribe
録音する
rokuonsuru

recover
治る
naoru

red
赤い
akai

refrigerator
冷蔵庫
reezooko

refugees
難民
nanmin

regarding to ~
(~に)関する
(~ni) kan suru

register
登録する
tooroku suru

reissue
再発行
saihakkoo

reject/ refuse
ことわる
kotowaru

relationship
関係
kankee

relatives
親戚
shinseki

release
解放する
kaihoo suru

religion
宗教
shuukyoo

remainder
のこり
nokori

remains/ruins
遺跡
iseki

remember
思い出す
omoidasu

remodel
改装する
kaisoo suru

rent
家賃
yachin

repair
直す
naosu

repair plant
修理工場
shuuri koojoo

repeat
くり返す
kurikaesu

reply/answer
返事
henji

report/document
申告
shinkoku

request
たのむ
tanomu

research
研究する
kenkyuu suru

reserved seat
指定席
shiteeseki

resident visa
居住ビザ
kyojuu biza

respect
尊敬
sonkee

responsibility
責任
sekinin

restriction/limit
制限
seegen

result
結果
kekka

result
検査
kensa

results/grades
成績
seeseki

retailing
小売り
kouri

retire
退職
taishoku

return
返す
kaesu

return something (store/company)
返品する
henpin suru

return/go home
帰る
kaeru

revolution
革命
kakumee

rice
米
kome

rice cooker
炊飯器
suihanki

rice field
たんぼ
tanbo

rice plant
稲
ine

rice porridge/gruel
粥
kayu

rich
金持ち
kanemochi

rich
ゆたか
yutaka

right
権利
kenri

right
右
migi

ring
指輪
yubiwa

ripe
熟す
jukusu

river
川
kawa

road/street
道
michi

roll
巻く
maku

roof
屋根
yane

room
部屋
heya

rot
腐る
kusaru

rough
荒い/粗い
arai/arai

round
まるい
marui

round trip
往復
oofuku

rubber band
輪ゴム
wagomu

rule
規則
kisoku

run
走る
hashiru

S

sad
悲しい
kanashii

safety
安全
anzen

sake
酒
sake

salary
給料
kyuuryoo

sales goods
商品
shoohin

salt
塩
shio

same
同じ
onaji

sample
見本
mihon

sand
砂
suna

sanitary pad
生理ナプキン
seiri napukin

sashimi/raw fish
刺身
sashimi

Saturday
土曜日
doyoo bi

save money/be thrifty
節約する
setsuyaku suru

say
言う
iu

scale
はかり
hakari

scary
こわい
kowai

scenery
景色
keshiki

scholar
学者
gakusha

school
学校
gakkoo

school entrance
入学
nyuugaku

science
科学
kagaku

scissors
はさみ
hasami

scold
しかる
shikaru

scotch tape
セロテープ
seroteepu

sculpture
彫刻
chookoku

sea
海
umi

sea mail
船便
funabin

sea shore
海岸
kaigan

seal
印鑑
inkan

sea-sick
船酔い
funayoi

season
季節
kisetsu

seasoning
調味料
choomiryoo

seat
席
seki

secret
秘密
himitsu

secretary
秘書
hisho

see
見る
miru

seed/pit
タネ
tane

selfish
勝手な、わがまま
kattena,wagamama

sell
売る
uru

send
送る
okuru

send a gift
贈る
okuru

send by mail
郵送する
yuusoo suru

sender
差出人
sashidashi nin

sense/feeling
感覚
kankaku

separate fees
別料金
betsu ryookin

September
9月
ku gatsu

serious
まじめ
majime

service charge
サービス料
saabisu ryoo

set down/in place
置く
oku

seven
7
shichi/nana

sew
縫う
nuu

sewing machine
ミシン
mishin

sex/gender
性
see

shadow
影
kage

shake hands
握手する
akushu suru

shallow
浅い
asai

shape
形
katachi

share a room
相部屋
aibeya

shark
サメ
same

sharp/pointed
するどい
surudoi

shave
剃る
soru

shelf
棚
tana

shell
貝
kai

shirt
シャツ
shatsu

shoes
クツ
kutsu

shop
店
mise

shop assistant
店員
ten in

shopping
買い物
kaimono

shore/bank/coast
岸
kishi

short
みじかい
mijikai

short cut
近道
chikamichi

short sleeves
半袖
hansode

short temper
短気
tanki

short term
短期
tanki

shorten
ちぢむ
chijimu

shorts
半ズボン
hanzubon

shoulder
肩
kata

shout
さけぶ
sakebu

show
見せる
miseru

show off
自慢する
jiman suru

shrimp
エビ
ebi

sibling
兄弟
kyoodai

signboard
看板
kanban

silk
絹
kinu

silver
銀
gin

simple
単純
tanjun

sin
罪
tsumi

sing
歌う
utau

singer
歌手
kashu

single/unmarried
未婚
mikon

sink
しずむ
shizumu

sisters
姉妹
shimai

sit
すわる
suwaru

size
大きさ
ookisa

skin
皮膚
hifu

skin disease
皮膚病
hifubyoo

skin/leather
皮、革
kawa

skirt
スカート
sukaato

sky
空
sora

skyscraper
高層ビル
koosoo biru

slacks
ズボン
zubon

sleep
寝る
neru

sleeping pill
睡眠薬
suimin yaku

sleepy
ねむい
nemui

sleeve cuff
ソデ(服)
sode(fuku)

slide down
すべる
suberu

sloppy
いいかげん
iikagen

slowly
ゆっくり
yukkuri

small
ちいさい
chiisai

small bird
小鳥
kotori

small change
小銭
kozeni

small intestine
小腸
shoocho

small pieces
粒
tsubu

smart
かしこい
kashikoi

smell/scent
香り
kaori

smile
笑顔
egao

smoke
けむり
kemuri

snake
ヘビ
hebi

sneakers
スニーカー
suniikaa

snore
いびきをかく
ibiki o kaku

snow
雪
yuki

soap
せっけん
sekken

society
社会
shakai

socks
くつした
kutsushita

soft
やわらかい
yawarakai

soft drinks
清涼飲料
seeryoo inryoo

soldier
軍人
gunjin

solve
解決する
kaiketsu suru

son
息子
musuko

song
歌
uta

soon
すぐに
suguni

sound
音
oto

sour
すっぱい
suppai

south
南
minami

Southeast Asia
東南アジア
toonan ajia

souvenir
みやげ
miyage

souvenir shop
みやげ物屋
miyagemonoya

soy sauce
しょうゆ
shooyu

space
宇宙
uchuu

spacious
広い
hiroi

special
特別
tokubetsu

special character
特徴
tokuchoo

spend thrift
ムダづかい
mudazukai

spicy
辛い
karai

spider
クモ
kumo

spinal cord
せきずい
sekizui

spirit
霊
ree

spirit/soul
精神
seeshin

splendid
すばらしい
subarashii

sports ground
競技場
kyoogijoo

sprain
ネンザする
nenza suru

spring
春
haru

square
四角
shikaku

squid
イカ
ika

stage
舞台
butai

stairs/steps
階段
kaidan

stamp
切手
kitte

stand
立つ
tatsu

standard
標準
hyoojun

star
星
hoshi

stare at
見つめる
mitsumeru

start from a destination
出発する
shuppatsu suru

starting time
出発時間
shuppatsu jikan

station
駅
eki

station close to you
最寄りの駅
moyori no eki

stationary store
文房具屋
bunbooguya

stay overnight
泊まる
tomaru

stay/reside
滞在する
taizai suru

steal
盗む
nusumu

sterile
衛生的
eeseeteki

sterilize (a wound)
消毒する
shoodoku suru

stick
棒
boo

stick together
くっつく
kuttsuku

stiff/hard
硬い
katai

stink/smell bad
くさい
kusai

stomach
胃
i

stomach ache
腹痛
fukutsuu

stomach medicine
胃腸薬
ichoo yaku

stone
石
ishi

stop
中止する
chuushi suru

stop
止まる
tomaru

straight
まっすぐ
massugu

strange
ヘンな
henna

strange/odd
奇妙な
kimyoo na

strange/unusual
不思議
fushigi

street
通り
toori

strength
力
chikara

string/thread
糸
ito

stripes
縞
shima

strong
つよい
tsuyoi

strong point
長所
choosho

strong/sturdy
じょうぶ
joobu

student
学生
gakusee

study
勉強する
benkyoo suru

study abroad
留学
ryuugaku

study/major
専攻
senkoo

stupid/fool
バカ
baka

suburb
郊外
koogai

suddenly
突然
totsuzen

suffer
悩む
nayamu

sufficient
たりる
tariru

sugar
砂糖
satoo

suit
スーツ
suutsu

summer
夏
natsu

summer vacation
夏休み
natsu yasumi

sunburn
日焼け
hiyake

sun screen
日焼け止めクリーム
hiyakedome kuriimu

sunrise
日の出
hinode

sunset
日の入り
hinoiri

superstition
迷信
meeshin

surgery
外科
geka

surprise
おどろく
odoroku

suspect (in a crime)
犯人
hannin

suspicious
あやしい
ayashii

sway
震える
furueru

sweet
あまい
amai

sweets
菓子
kashi

swim
泳ぐ
oyogu

swimming
水泳
suiei

swimming suit
水着
mizugi

symptom
症状
shoojoo

T

take a rest
休む
yasumu

take a walk
散歩する
sanpo suru

take off (clothes)
脱ぐ
nugu

talent
才能
sainoo

talk
話す
hanasu

tall (height)
高い(高さ)
takai (takasa)

tap water
水道水
suidoosui

taste
味見する
ajimi suru

taste/seasoning
味
aji

tastes bad
まずい
mazui

tattoo
イレズミ
irezumi

tax
税金
zeekin

taxi stand
タクシー乗り場
takushii noriba

tea
茶
cha

tea cup
茶わん
chawan

teach
教える
oshieru

teacher
先生
sensee

tear
なみだ
namida

tease
いたずら
itazura

technical college
専門学校
senmongakkoo

tee shirt
Tシャツ
T-shatsu

telephone
電話
denwa

telephone area code
市外局番
shigai kyokuban

telephone directory
電話帳
denwachoo

telephone number
電話番号
denwabangoo

telescope
望遠鏡
booenkyoo

temperature
温度
ondo

temple
寺院
ji in

terrible
ひどい(状態)
hidoi (joo tai)

test
試験
shiken

tetanus
破傷風
hashoofuu

texture
生地
kiji

thank
感謝する
kansha suru

that
あの
ano

that
あれ
are

that time
あの頃
anokoro

that/it
それ
sore

the best
最高
saikoo

the day after tomorrow
あさって
asatte

the day before
おととい
ototoi

the other day
先日
sen jitsu

the other side
向こう側
mukoo gawa

the West
西欧
seeoo

theater
劇場
gekijoo

theft
盗難
toonan

theft report
盗難届
toonan todoke

then
そして
soshite

there
あそこ
asoko

thermometer
体温計
taionkee

thermos
水筒
suitoo

they
彼ら
karera

thick
厚い
atsui

thief
泥棒
doroboo

thin
うすい
usui

think
思う
omou

this
この
kono

this month
今月
kon getsu

this morning
今朝
kesa

this time
今回
konkai

this week
今週
konshuu

this year
今年
kotoshi

those/them
それら
sorera

thousand
千
sen

throat
のど
nodo

throw
投げる
nageru

throw away
すてる
suteru

thumb
親指
oyayubi

Thursday
木曜日
mokuyoobi

ticket sales window
切符売り場
kippu uriba

tie
結ぶ
musubu

tiger
トラ
tora

tight/hard
きつい
kitsui

tighten
しばる
shibaru

time
時間
jikan

~time
～回
~kai

time at a site
現地時間
genchi jikan

time difference
時差
jisa

time period
期間
kikan

time period
期限
kigen

time table
時刻表
jikokuhyoo

~times
～倍
~bai

to ~ (destination)
～行き
~iki

today
今日
kyoo

tofu
豆腐
toofu

together
いっしょ
issho

toll road
有料道路
yuuryoo dooro

tomorrow
明日
ashita

tongue
舌
shita

tonight
今晩
konban

tonsillitis
扁桃腺
hentoosen

too bad
残念
zannen

tooth
歯
ha

tooth brush
ハブラシ
haburashi

tooth paste
ハミガキ粉
hamigakiko

touch
さわる
sawaru

tourism
観光
kankoo

tourist
観光客
kankookyaku

tourist attraction/area
観光地
kankoochi

towel
タオル
taoru

tower
塔
too

town
町
machi

toy
おもちゃ
omocha

trade
貿易
booeki

tradition
伝統的
dentoo teki

traffic
交通
kootsuu

traffic information
交通事故
kootsuu jiko

traffic signal
信号
shingoo

translate
通訳する、翻訳する
tsuuyaku suru,honyaku suru

transparent
透明な
toomee na

travel
旅行
ryokoo

travel agent
旅行代理店
ryokoo dairiten

treat/pay for
おごる
ogoru

tree
木
ki

triangle
三角
sankaku

trouble
迷惑
meewaku

truth
真実
shinjitsu

try hard
がんばる
ganbaru

try out
ためす
tamesu

tuberculosis
結核
kekkaku

Tuesday
火曜日
kayoobi

tuna
マグロ
maguro

turkey
七面鳥
shichimenchoo

turn off/to erase
消す
kesu

typhoon
台風
taifuu

U

umbrella
カサ
kasa

uncle
おじ
oji

under
下
shita

understand
わかる
wakaru

underwear
下着
shitagi

unemployed
失業する
shitsugyoo suru

unemployed
無職
mushoku

unhappy
不幸な
fukoona

unique
個性的
koseeteki

university
大学
daigaku

university student
大学生
daigakusee

urgent
急用
kyuuyoo

urine
尿
nyoo

usage fee
使用料
shiyooryoo

use
つかう
tsukau

used car
中古車
chuukosha

used clothing
古着
furugi

useful
役に立つ
yaku ni tatsu

useful/handy
便利
benri

uterus/womb
子宮
shikyuu

V

valid period
有効期限
yuukookigen

valley
谷
tani

valuables
貴重品
kichoohin

value
価値
kachi

vanish
消える
kieru

various
いろいろ
iroiro

vegetable
野菜
yasai

vegetarian
菜食主義
saishoku shugi

vehicle
乗り物
norimono

vending machine
自動販売機
jidoohanbaiki

vertical
縦
tate

vinegar
酢
su

violation/offense
違反
ihan

visit
訪れる
otozureru

visit a shrine/pray
お参りする
omairi suru

voice
声
koe

volcano
火山
kazan

voltage
電圧
den atsu

vomit
吐く
haku

W

wait
待つ
matsu

walk
あるく
aruku

wall
壁
kabe

wallet
サイフ
saifu

want/desire
欲しい
hoshii

ward
区
ku

warm
暖かい
atatakai

warm water
湯
yu

warning/caution
注意
chuui

warranty
保証書
hoshoosho

wash
洗う
arau

wash basin
洗面台
senmendai

water
水
mizu

water fountain
噴水
funsui

waterfall
滝
taki

waterworks
水道
suidoo

wave
波
nami

we
私たち
watashitachi

weak
弱い
yowai

weak (in taste)
薄い(味)
usui(ajii)

weak points
短所
tansho

wear
着る
kiru

wear shoes
履く
haku

weather
天気
tenki

weather report
天気予報
tenkiyohoo

weaving
織物
orimono

wedding ceremony
結婚式
kekkon shiki

Wednesday
水曜日
suiyoobi

week
週
shuu

weight
体重、重さ
taijuu,omosa

west
西
nishi

wet
しめった
shimetta

wet towel
おしぼり
oshibori

whale
クジラ
kujira

wheat
小麦
komugi

wheel chair
車イス
kurumaisu

white
白
shiro

wife
妻
tsuma

win
勝つ
katsu

wind
風
kaze

window
窓
mado

wing
羽
hane

winter
冬
fuyu

wipe
拭く
fuku

woman
女性
josee

wonderful
立派
rippa

word
ことば
kotoba

work
はたらく
hataraku

working visa
労働ビザ
roodoo biza

worry
心配する
shinpai suru

worst
最悪
saiaku

wound
傷
kizu

wrapping
包装
hoosoo

wring
しぼる
shiboru

write
書く
kaku

Y

yellow
黄色
kiiro

yesterday
昨日
kinoo

you
あなた
anata

young
若い
wakai

younger brother
弟
otooto

younger sister
妹
imooto

youngest child
末っ子
suekko

youth
青年
seenen

Z

Zen Buddhism
禅
zen

zoo
動物園
doobutsuen

おかげさまで510万部突破！　大好評の

【旅の指さし会話帳】

1	タイ［第三版］	1,400円	34	ハワイ	1,300円
2	インドネシア［第三版］	1,400円	35	フィンランド	1,800円
3	香港［第三版］	1,400円	36	チェコ	1,800円
4	中国［第三版］	1,400円	37	上海	1,400円
5	韓国［第三版］	1,400円	38	シンガポール	1,500円
6	イタリア［第三版］	1,400円	39	エジプト	1,700円
7	オーストラリア［第二版］	1,300円	40	アルゼンチン	1,700円
8	台湾［第二版］	1,300円	41	アフガニスタン	1,600円
9	アメリカ［第二版］	1,300円	42	北朝鮮	1,700円
10	イギリス［第二版］	1,300円	43	ニューヨーク	1,400円
11	ベトナム［第二版］	1,500円	44	ミャンマー	1,800円
12	スペイン［第四版］	1,400円	45	北京	1,400円
13	キューバ	1,700円	46	イラク	1,800円
14	フィリピン［第二版］	1,400円	47	モロッコ	1,800円
15	マレーシア［第二版］	1,400円	48	オーストリア	1,700円
16	モンゴル	1,700円	49	ハンガリー	1,800円
17	フランス［第二版］	1,300円	50	ルーマニア	1,800円
18	トルコ［第二版］	1,500円	51	アイルランド	1,800円
19	カンボジア［第二版］	1,800円	52	ポルトガル	1,700円
20	ドイツ［第二版］	1,300円	53	ジャマイカ	1,800円
21	JAPAN【英語版】	1,500円	54	ニュージーランド	1,500円
22	インド	1,500円	55	モルディブ	1,800円
23	ブラジル	1,500円	56	スリランカ	1,800円
24	ギリシア	1,500円	57	ノルウェー	1,800円
25	ネパール	1,800円	58	ポーランド	1,800円
26	ロシア	1,700円	59	西安	1,600円
27	JAPAN【韓国語版】	1,500円	60	ケニア	1,800円
28	メキシコ	1,600円	61	グアム	1,300円
29	オランダ	1,600円	62	ペルー	1,700円
30	スウェーデン	1,800円	63	雲南	1,600円
31	デンマーク	1,800円	64	ラオス	1,800円
32	カナダ	1,500円	65	チベット	1,800円
33	JAPAN【中国語（北京語）版】	1,500円	66	ベルギー	1,500円

「旅の指さし会話帳シリーズ」一覧

67	KYOTO【京ことば】	1,500円
68	サイパン	1,300円
69	JAPAN【スペイン語版】	1,500円
70	タヒチ	1,800円
71	スイス	1,600円
72	イラン	1,800円
73	クロアチア	1,800円
74	バリ	1,300円
75	パキスタン	1,800円
76	南インド	1,800円
77	チュニジア	1,800円
78	ドバイ	1,500円
79	JAPON【フランス語版】	1,500円
80	スロバキア	1,800円
81	ブータン	1,800円
82	イスラエル	1,800円

【ビジネス指さし会話帳】

1	中国語	1,500円
2	英語	1,500円
3	タイ	1,500円
4	台湾華語	1,500円
5	韓国語	1,500円

【食べる指さし会話帳】

1	タイ	1,200円
2	韓国	1,200円
3	ベトナム［第二版］	1,500円
4	台湾	1,500円
5	中国	1,500円
6	フランス	1,500円
7	イタリア	1,500円
8	インドネシア	1,700円
9	JAPANESE FOOD	1,500円

【遊ぶ指さし会話帳】

ダイビング（英語）	1,500円

【恋する指さし会話帳】

1	英語編	1,400円
2	フランス語編	1,500円
3	フィリピン語編	1,800円
4	韓国語編	1,500円
5	インドネシア語編	1,500円

【旅の指さし会話帳　国内編】

1	沖縄	1,400円
2	大阪	1,400円

【暮らしの日本語指さし会話帳】

1	フィリピン語版	1,500円
2	ポルトガル語版	1,500円
3	中国語版	1,500円
4	英語版	1,500円
5	韓国語版	1,500円
6	スペイン語版	1,500円

【旅の指さし会話帳 mini】

●韓国　●台北　●イタリア
●中国　●上海　●フランス
●タイ　●バリ　●スペイン
●香港　●ハワイ　●ドイツ
●ベトナム　●グアム　●英語

各680円

● JAPAN

【英語・中国語・韓国語・スペイン語・フランス語】　各680円

●いきなり出張会話

【中国・韓国・タイ・英語】各800円

価格はすべて税別

カバーイラスト　むろふしかえ
本文イラスト　朝倉千夏、むろふしかえ
ブックデザイン　斉藤いづみ［rhyme inc.］
本文 DTP　赤地崇一
企画協力　株式会社エビデンス

旅の指さし会話帳 mini JAPAN（English Edition）

2010 年 7 月 17 日　第 1 刷
2019 年 4 月 3 日　第 5 刷

監修　ヘンリー・ドレナン
発行者　田村隆英
発行所　株式会社情報センター出版局
〒 160-0004　東京都新宿区四谷 2-1 四谷ビル
電話 03-3358-0231　振替 00140-4-46236
URL:http://www.4jc.co.jp　http://www.yubisashi.com

EVIDENCE CORPORATION

印刷　モリモト印刷株式会社

ISBN978-4-7958-4223-6

Fill-in Format!

Show and Speak Book!

Jot down names and addresses of shops, things you want to buy and/or eat.

I want to go to~.
～に行きたいです
ni ikitai desu

1 yen 一円
ichi en

5 yen 五円
go en

10 yen 十円
juu en

I often receive as small change. I want to use them so that they won't pile up.
おつりでもらうことが多い。すぐたまるのでこまめに使おう。

50 yen 五十円
gojuu en

Widely used domestic postcard is 50 yen.
日本国内で使える、一般的な郵便はがきが50円。

100 yen 百円
hyaku en

Chewing gum, icecream, rice-balls are about 100 yen.
ガムやアイス、おにぎりなどがだいたい100円。

500 yen 五百円
gohyaku en

Beef on rice, Tako-Yaki, and light snacks are about 500 yen.
牛丼やたこ焼き、軽食などは500円前後で食べられる。

1,000 yen 千円
sen en

Paper money is easier to use, fit for all occasions.
シチュエーションを問わず、使い勝手のよい紙幣。

2,000 yen 弐千円
nisen en

Issued to commemorate the 2000 Okinawa G8 Summit.
2000年沖縄サミットを記念して発行。あまり流通していない。

5,000 yen 五千円
gosen en

Widely used for paying meals and for shopping.
夕食や買い物のときなどによく使う紙幣。

10,000 yen 壱万円
ichiman en

Not recommended using in small stores and taxis; they may not have change.
小さな店やタクシーなどで使うと、相手がおつりに困ることも。